2

Wonderful WORLD

SECOND EDITION

WORKBOOK

NATIONAL GEOGRAPHIC LEARNING

Australia · Brazil · Mexico · Singapore · United Kingdom · United States

NATIONAL GEOGRAPHIC

LEARNING

***Wonderful World 2* Workbook, Second Edition**

Vice President, Editorial Director: John McHugh
Executive Editor: Siân Mavor
Commissioning Editor: Kayleigh Buller
Senior Development Editor: Karen Haller Beer
Head of Strategic Marketing EMEA ELT: Charlotte Ellis
Product Marketing Executive: Ellen Setterfield
Head of Production and Design: Celia Jones
Content Project Manager: Melissa Beavis
Manufacturing Manager: Eyvett Davis
Cover Design: Lisa Trager
Interior Design and Composition: Lumina Datamatics, Inc.

Workbook: Level 2
ISBN: 978-1-4737-6062-2

National Geographic Learning
Cheriton House, North Way
Andover, Hampshire, SP10 5BE
United Kingdom

National Geographic Learning, a Cengage Learning Company, has a mission to bring the world to the classroom and the classroom to life. With our English language programs, students learn about their world by experiencing it. Through our partnerships with National Geographic and TED Talks, they develop the language and skills they need to be successful global citizens and leaders.

Locate your local office at **international.cengage.com/region**

Visit National Geographic Learning online at **NGL.Cengage.com/ELT**
Visit our corporate website at **www.cengage.com**

Printed in China by RR Donnelley
Print Number: 03 Print Year: 2019

Contents

Alphabet

1 Look and write.

A a

B b

C c

D __

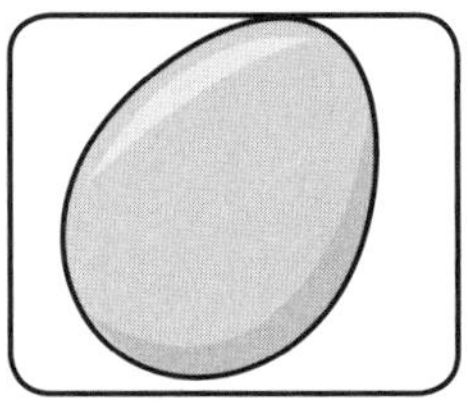

E e

F f

__ g

H h

I __

__ J

K k

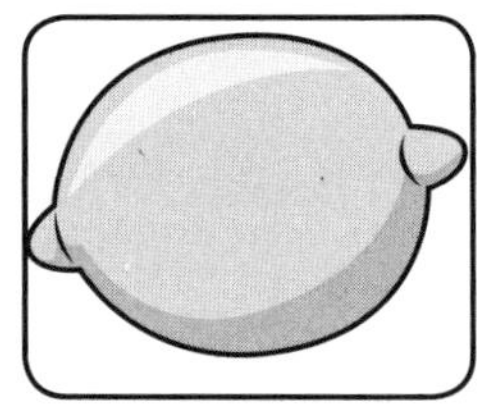

L l

M __

N n

O o

__ p

Q q

R __

S s

__ t

U u

V v

W w

X x

__ y

Z __

Numbers

1 Look and write.

1	2	____	4	5
one	two	three	four	five
6	7	____	9	10
six	seven	eight	nine	ten
11	12	13	14	____
eleven	twelve	thirteen	fourteen	fifteen
16	17	18	____	20
sixteen	seventeen	____	nineteen	twenty

2 Write.

1 I'm f o u r teen.

3 We're th ___ t ___ n.

5 We're e ___ ven.

2 I'm n ___ ___ ___.

4 I'm tw ___ ___ y.

6 I'm ___ x.

Colours

1 Read and colour.

1  red

2  black

3  green

4  pink

5  orange

6  blue

7  brown

8  purple

9  yellow

10  white

2 Look and colour.

Hello!

1 Match and say.

What's your name?

How old are you?

How are you?

Fine, thanks.

My name's Ana.

I'm twelve.

2 Read and sing.

What's your name? My name's Ana.
Where are you from? I'm from
Greece.
What's your name?
What's your name?

Are you Alex, José or Tim?
What's your name?
What's your name?
Are you Sara, Jane or Kim?

Boys and girls,
How are you?
Fine, thanks!
Fine, thanks!
How are you?

How old are you?
How old are you?
Are you nine or ten or two?
How old are you?
How old are you?
Are you twelve or twenty-two?

Family

1 Find and circle.

~~mum~~ dad brother sister baby aunt
uncle grandma grandpa cousin

O	N	O	G	P	A	U	N	T
C	S	B	R	O	T	H	E	R
F	P	D	A	C	A	B	D	C
G	R	A	N	D	M	A	U	O
F	V	D	D	B	U	B	N	U
D	E	F	P	D	M	Y	C	S
B	N	D	A	F	N	U	L	I
S	I	S	T	E	R	E	E	N

2 Read and draw.

This is my family...

Days of the Week and Time

1 **Write.**

2 Tu _ s _ _ _

3 W _ dn _ s _ _ _

4 T _ ur _ _ _ _

5 F _ i _ _ _

6 S _ _ ur _ _ _

7 S _ n _ _ _

2 **Match.**

It's midnight. ~~It's two o'clock.~~ It's eight o'clock. It's midday.
It's four o'clock. It's ten o'clock.

1 

It's two o'clock.

2 

____

3 

____

4 

____

5 

____

6 

____

Seasons

1 Write and colour.

~~spring~~ summer autumn winter

1

spring

2

____

3

____

4

____

Plurals

1 Write.

baby child ~~foot~~ penguin snake tomato

1

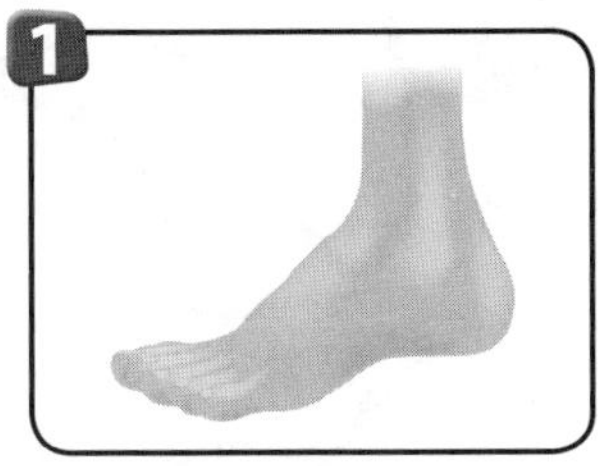

foot

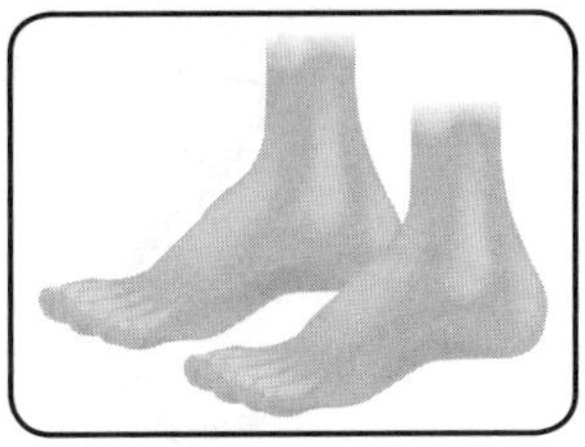

feet

4

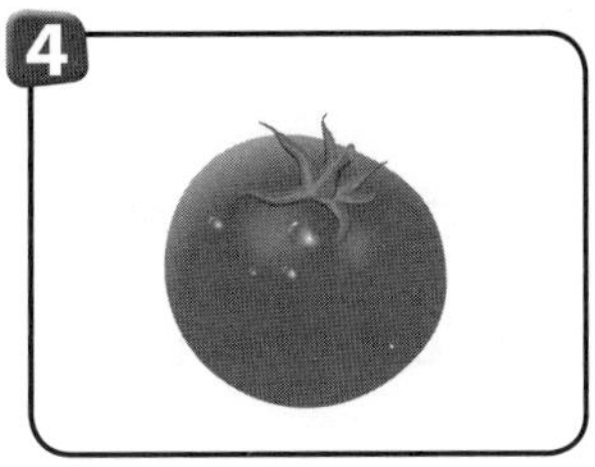

2

5

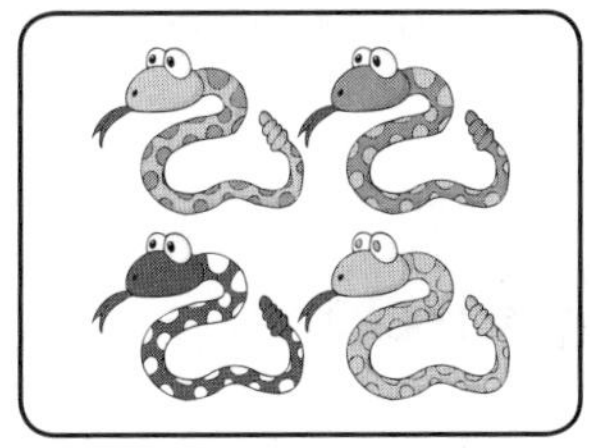

3

6

A, An, The and This, That, These, Those

1 Circle and colour.

1 There is **a** / **an** ant in the garden. **The** / **A** ant is brown.

2 We went to the zoo. We saw **a** / **an** octopus, **a** / **an** lion and **a** / **an** elephant!

3 Look at **a** / **the** sea! There are lots of boats.

2 Circle.

This / **These** apples are red!

Those / **That** parrots are beautiful!

That / **This** robot is cool!

These / **Those** cars are fantastic!

This / **That** isn't my football!

Those / **That** is my grandpa.

In the Classroom

1 Write.

in groups   your homework   hand up   ~~up~~   down
be quiet   the board   your book

1 Stand ___up___
2 Open ______
3 Work ______
4 Please ______
5 Put your ______
6 Sit ______
7 Go to ______
8 Take out ______

2 Colour.

1 On the Farm

Lesson 1

1 Write.

1 s h e e p
2 _ _ _ _ _ _ _ _
3 _ _ _ _ _
4 _ _ _
5 _ _ _ _
6 _ _ _ _

2 Match and colour.

The baby duck is yellow.
The cow is black and white.
The horse is black.
The chicken is red and orange.
The sheep is white.
The goat is brown.

3 Write *have got* or *has got*.

1 The duck has got two wings.
2 My cows ________ black and white legs.
3 That goat ________ yellow eyes.
4 The farm ________ five horses.
5 The sheep ________ plenty of food.
6 My mum and dad ________ a pet chicken.

4 Write.

He's got She's got I've got They've got They've got ~~We've got~~

1

We've got a black horse.

4

__________ a new dog.

2

__________ four white goats.

5

__________ a big farm.

3

__________ a sheep on my T-shirt!

6

__________ lots of chickens.

5 Write and say.

Emily

Martin

Rachel

Alice

Paul

Peter

1 She's got a parrot. It's Emily.

2 He's got a cool hat. __________

3 She's got a horse. __________

4 He's got a lizard. __________

5 She's got flowers. __________

6 He's got a cow. __________

Lesson 2

1 Match.

1 

2 

3 

grow
farmer
field
grass
pizza
tractor

4 

5 

6 

2 Write.

pizza ~~farmer~~ tractor field grow grass

My uncle is a (1) farmer. Lots of plants (2) ______ on his farm. He's got cows and horses, too. The horses have got a big (3) ______ to run in. They eat (4) ______. I like riding on the red (5) ______. It's fun! My aunt makes a (6) ______ for dinner with the cheese and tomatoes from the farm. It's delicious!

3 Circle.

1 My aunt **haven't got** / **hasn't got** a goat.

2 My mum and dad **haven't got** / **hasn't got** a tractor.

3 I **haven't got** / **hasn't got** a horse.

4 The farm **haven't got** / **hasn't got** a river on it.

5 My friends **haven't got** / **hasn't got** a farm.

6 The pizza **haven't got** / **hasn't got** tomatoes on it.

4 Read and write.

1 Wendy and I have got a dog. We haven't got a duck. (duck)
2 My uncle's got a nice farm. ______. (garden)
3 I've got an aunt. ______. (uncle)
4 The farm has got lots of fields. ______. (trees)
5 Lucy has got a brother. ______. (sister)
6 My mum and dad have got a car. ______. (tractor)

5 Write and say.

chicken chicken got sheep sheep
~~moo~~ baa cow cow cluck

What animal am I?
Moo, moo, moo.
What animal am I?

I'm a ______.
I'm a big, brown ______.
I've ______ big eyes and a nice, long tail!
I make milk for you to drink!

What animal am I?
Baa, ______, baa.
What animal am I?

I'm a ______. I'm a small, black ______.
I've got black hair and four short legs!
I make wool for your jumpers!

What animal am I?
Cluck, ______, cluck.
What animal am I?

I'm a ______. I'm a short,
white ______.
I've got two wings and two small feet!
I make eggs for you to eat!

Lesson 3

1 Circle and write.

t s w o r k t c p i c k l e u w a t e r b r i p l a n t a c k f e e d z y c d i g

1 

work

3 

____

5 

____

2 

____

4 

____

6 

____

2 Write.

digs waters ~~works~~ picks plants feeds

1 My Dad works on a farm.

2 He __________ the animals every day.

3 In the spring, Dad __________ in the field.

4 He __________ the tomato seeds and they grow.

5 Dad __________ the tomato plants every day.

6 When they're ready, Dad __________ the tomatoes and we can eat them!

3 Match.

1 Have you got a tractor?
2 Have goats got wings?
3 Has Tara got a big pizza?
4 Have you and Ben got a pet horse?
5 Has the farmer got a field?
6 Has the duck got yellow feet?

a No, she hasn't.
b Yes, I have.
c Yes, he has.
d Yes, it has.
e No, they haven't.
f No, we haven't.

4 Circle.

1 **Has** / **have** the farm got a river on it?
No, it **has** / **hasn't**.
2 **Have** / **Hasn't** your mum and dad got a car?
No, they **have** / **haven't**.
3 **Have** / **Has** your garden got lots of grass?
Yes, it **have** / **has**.
4 **Have** / **has** Mary and Matthew got pets?
Yes, they **have** / **hasn't**.
5 **Have** / **Has** you got a red and black chicken?
No, I **have** / **haven't**.
6 **Hasn't** / **Has** the farmer got a brother?
Yes, she **hasn't** / **has**.

5 Write and say. Draw.

This is my farm.
I've got ____________.

I feed the ____________
in the morning.

I water the ____________
at night.

I haven't got ____________.

2 Family Time

Lesson 1

1 Match.

twins
son
daughter
wife
husband

2 Write.

son wife daughters twins ~~husband~~

My aunt Maria and her (1) husband, Jim have got four children. They've got three (2) ______, Jane, Liz and Lucy. Liz and Lucy are 12 years old. They're (3) ______. Maria and Jim have got a (4) ______, too. His name is Mike and he's 20. His (5) ______ is called Ana.

3 Circle.

1 Maria (**is**) / **are** Jim's wife.
2 Liz and Lucy **is** / **are** twins.
3 Jane **is** / **are** Maria's daughter.
4 Mike **is** / **are** Ana's husband.
5 I **am** / **are** Mike's cousin.
6 Jane, Liz and Lucy **is** / **are** Mike's sisters.

4 Write.

1 Jane, Liz and Lucy are sisters.

They're sisters.

2 Lucy and I are cousins.

_____________ cousins.

3 Ana is Mike's wife.

_____________ Mike's wife.

4 I am Mike's cousin.

_____________ Mike's cousin.

5 Jim is Maria's husband.

_____________ Maria's husband.

6 You are my friend.

_____________ my friend.

5 Write *is* or *are*. Colour.

Mike's hair (1) 's black.
His shoes (2) _____________ brown.
His trousers (3) _____________ blue and
his T-shirt (4) _____________ green.

Ana's dress (5) _____________
orange. She's got nice boots.
They (6) _____________ black.
Her hair (7) _____________ brown
and her hat (8) _____________ pink.

Lesson 2

1 Circle.

1 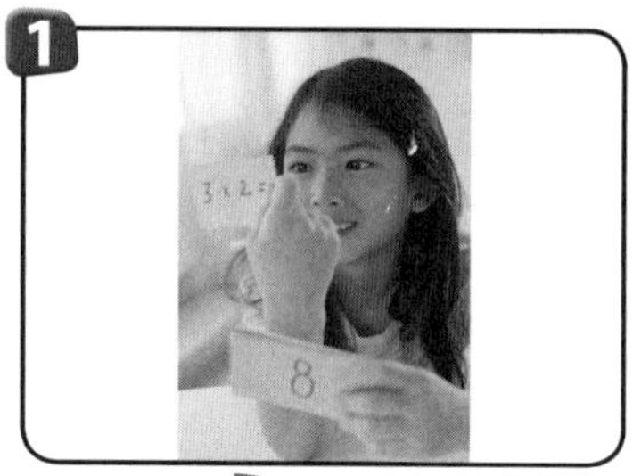

clever / cute

3 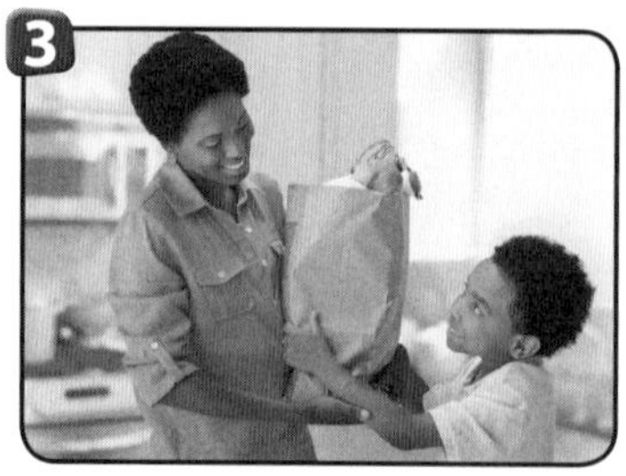

naughty / help

5 

cute / clever

2 

naughty / help

4 

help / good

6 

kind / clever

2 Write.

clever help cute naughty good ~~kind~~

1 

My dog Spot is kind. He likes to ______ my mum.

3 

Spot can catch a ball. He is very ______.

5 

Spot can be ______, too. He digs in the garden and my mum doesn't like it.

2 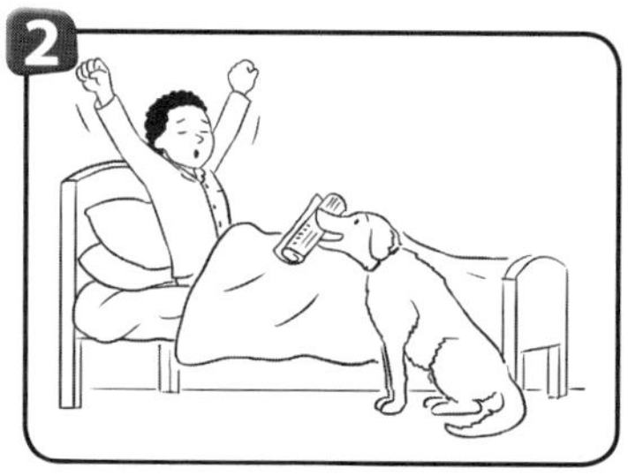

Spot isn't always naughty. He is a ______ dog in the morning.

4 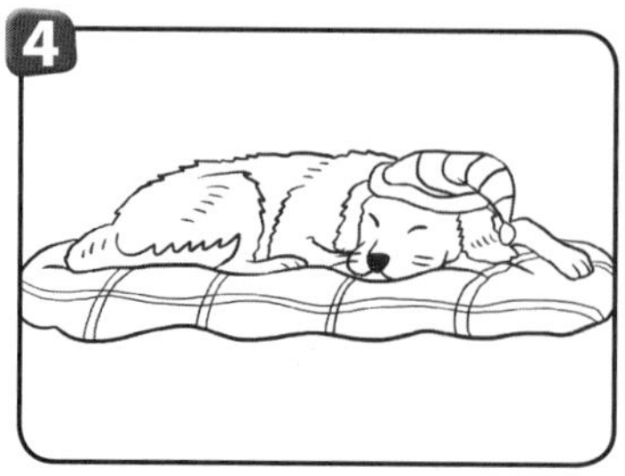

Look at Spot! He is very ______.

3 Write.

1 Your dog is naughty. __It isn't__ good.

2 She's my sister. ____________ my cousin.

3 We're cousins. ____________ twins.

4 The goat is cute. ____________ ugly.

5 I'm tall. ____________ short.

6 They don't help me. ____________ kind.

4 Match.

It isn't a cow.
I'm not seven years old.
We aren't on a farm.
You aren't my dad.
She isn't my aunt.

5 Write and sing.

~~He isn't~~	They aren't	I'm not	She isn't	I'm not

My brother is naughty! Yes, he is!
He isn't good! __He isn't__ kind!
My brother is naughty! Oh, what can I do?

My sister is naughty! Yes, she is!
She isn't good! ____________ kind!
My sister is naughty! Oh, what can I do?

My cousins are naughty! Yes, they are!
They aren't good! ____________ kind!
My cousins are naughty! Oh, what can I do?

I'm not naughty! No, ____________!
I'm so good! I'm so kind!
____________ naughty! I'm so good!

Lesson 3

1 Write.

yrgna angry

pphay ________

asd ________

nuyghr ________

srythit ________

redit ________

2 Write.

thirsty hungry ~~tired~~ happy sad angry

1 Amy plays a lot of football. She is tired.

2 John wants to drink some water. He's ________.

3 That goat is eating our plants. My Dad is very ________.

4 I'm ________. I want a sandwich.

5 My brother has a new toy car. He's very ________.

6 The dog can't play in the garden. It is ________.

3 Circle.

1 Is this a pizza?

Yes, **I am** / **it is**.

2 Are the twins hungry?

No, **it isn't** / **they aren't**.

3 Are those girls your daughters?

Yes, **she is** / **they are**.

4 Is your son in the photo?

Yes, **he is** / **you are**.

5 Are you sad?

No, **I'm not** / **you aren't**.

6 Is your teacher tired?

No, **she isn't** / **we aren't**.

4 Write.

1 Are the girls hungry? Yes, they are.

2 Are the girls sad? ______________________

3 Are the girls twins? ______________________

5 Read, circle and say.

1

Is he thirsty?
No, he isn't.
He's **angry / hungry**.

hungry

2

Is he happy?
No, he isn't.
He's **thirsty / angry**.

____

3

Are they sad?
No, they aren't.
They're **happy / tired**.

____

4

Are they
angry / happy?
Yes, they are!

____

Review 1 Units 1–2

1 Write.

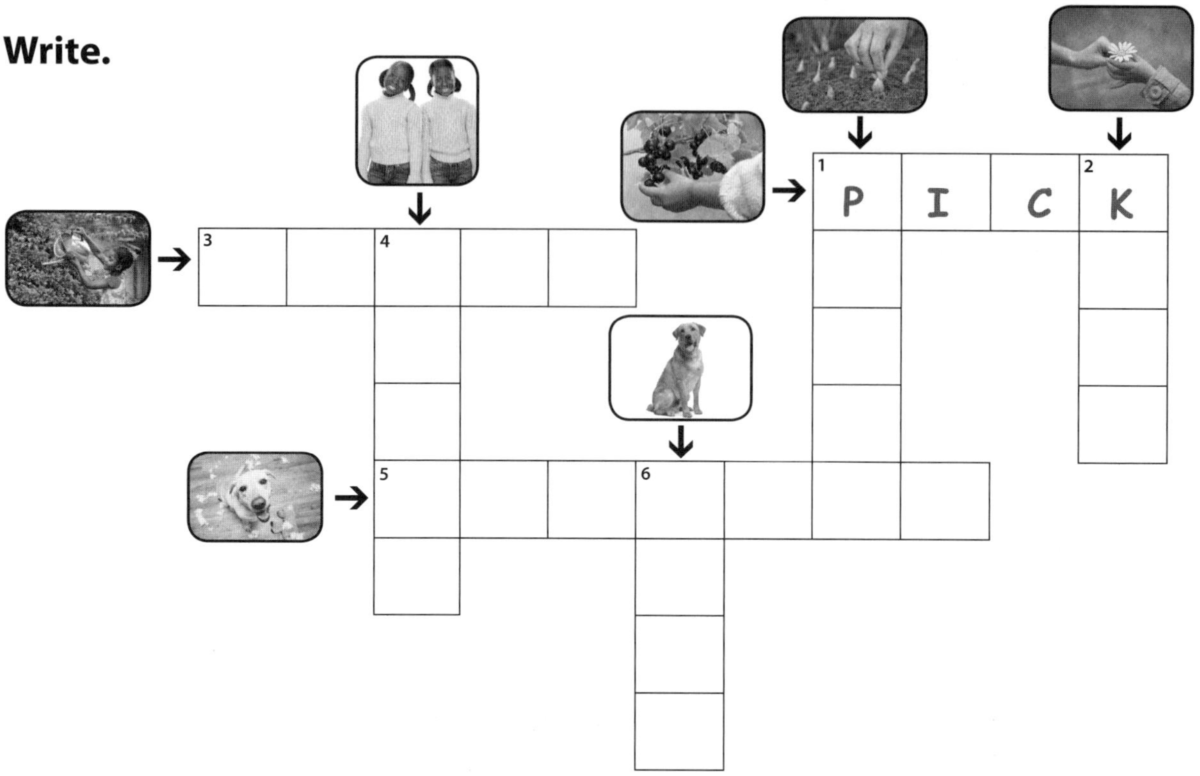

2 Circle.

1 This is my **tractor** / **son**, John.

2 Are they your **cows** / **duck?** Yes, they are.

3 The farm has got a big **field** / **tomato**.

4 Your **daughter** / **pizza** is very clever.

5 My dad **feeds** / **digs** the goats every day.

6 Your horse is **thirsty** / **cute**. It wants some water.

3 Write.

1 Is the dog cute?

Yes, it is.

2 Are the boys brothers?

Yes, they ______.

3 Are the boys sad?

No, they ______.

4 Write.

1 Have you got a tractor? No, I haven't (✗).

2 Katie ______ (✗) a chicken. She's got a horse.

3 Ben ______ (✔) a new T-shirt. It's black.

4 The farm ______ (✔) a field. It's big.

5 ______ Harry ______ a pet goat? Yes, ______. (✔)

6 A sheep ______ (✗) wings. It's got four legs.

5 Read and draw. Say.

How are you?

3 At Home

Lesson 1

1 Look and circle.

1 wall / door
2 dining room / table
3 window / stairs
4 wall / dining room
5 table / stairs
6 window / door

2 Write.

1 This 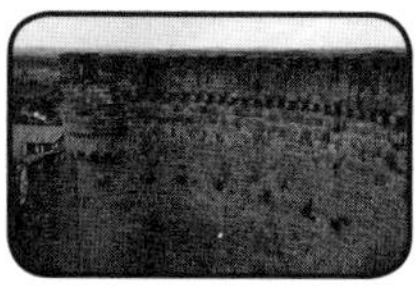 ___wall___ is very old.

2 We eat dinner in the  ________.

3 That house has got a blue  ________.

4 There's a new  ________ in the kitchen.

5 They are on the  ________.

6 This  ________ is very big.

3 Write *There's, There isn't, There are* or *There aren't*.

1 

There isn't a dog in the park.

2 

__________ some apples on the table.

3 

__________ any cows in the field.

4 

__________ a big window in the dining room.

5 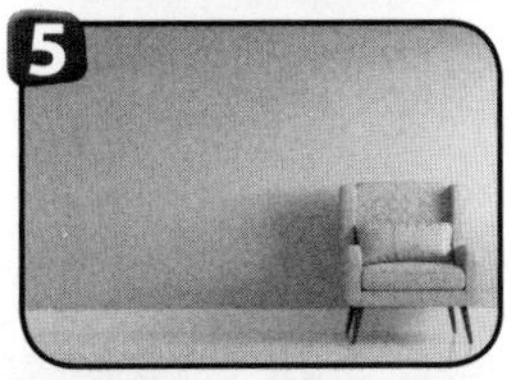

__________ a door in the wall.

6 

__________ a bird in the tree.

4 Write.

1 Is there a table in the dining room? Yes, there is.

2 __________ goats on the farm? No, __________.

3 __________ stairs in the house? Yes, __________.

4 __________ a cinema? No, __________.

5 __________ a book in your school bag? No, __________.

6 __________ flowers in the field? Yes, __________.

5 Read, draw and colour.

This is our dining room. There are two small windows and the stairs are brown. There's a door. It's yellow. There are pink flowers on the table. Our cat is on the table, too! It's orange.

Lesson 2

1 Circle and write.

fflloorwersleepfphmessyyyptbookshelfvdtoyboxtbtidyres

1 

toy box

3 

5 

2 

4 

6 

2 Look and tick.

1		bookshelf	☑	floor	☐
2		tidy	☐	messy	☐
3		sleep	☐	toy box	☐
4		toy box	☐	floor	☐
5	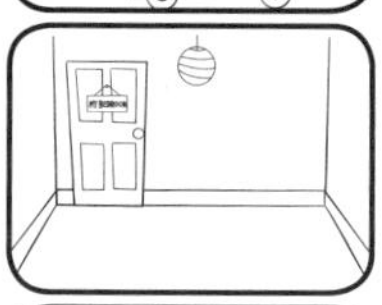	floor	☐	tidy	☐
6		sleep	☐	tidy	☐

3 Write.

1 This is ___my___ toy box. I put my toys in it. (I)

2 Is ________ rabbit cute? (you)

3 The elephant is small, but ________ ears are big. (it)

4 Are the twins in ________ bedroom? (they)

5 They have got ________ books. (we)

6 Is this ________ horse? (you)

4 Look and write.

Grandpa Emma Grandma Paul Jane Steve

1 Whose table is this? ___It's Grandpa's table___.

2 Whose tractor is this? ________________.

3 Whose toys are these? ________________.

4 Whose bookshelf is this? ________________.

5 Whose ducks are these? ________________.

6 Whose fish is this? ________________.

5 Draw and write.

My bedroom

1 ________________

2 ________________

3 ________________

Lesson 3

1 Write.

sink ~~fridge~~ far (from) between near sofa rug

1  ______fridge______.

2  ______________.

3  ______________.

4  ______________.

5  ______________.

6  ______________.

7  ______________.

2 Write and colour.

1 The fridge is ______near______ the window.
2 The ______________ is black.
3 The books are on the ______________.
4 The ______________ is on the rug.
5 The cat is ______________ the fridge and the sofa.
6 The flowers are in the ______________.
7 The door is ______________ the sink.

3 Circle.

1 There's a / **the** nice museum near my house.

2 I'm in **a** / **the** toy shop. **A** / **The** shop's got beautiful dolls.

3 He's got **a** / **the** rug in his dining room. **A** / **The** rug is new.

4 **A** / **The** window isn't very big.

5 It's **a** / **the** nice house, but it's far from the library.

6 It's **a** / **an** elephant, it isn't **a** / **an** monkey.

4 Circle and match.

a 

c 

e 

b 

d 

f 

1 There's a / **an** cute sheep! b

2 **An** / **The** dog is very good! ☐

3 There's **a** / **an** cow. ☐

4 That is **a** / **an** new door. ☐

5 **An** / **The** clock is big! ☐

6 There's a bird in **a** / **the** tree! ☐

5 Match and say.

1	Look! A horse!	a	The tractor is really big.
2	Look! Goats!	b	The farmer is really kind.
3	Look! A tractor!	c	The horse is in the field.
4	Look! Apples!	d	The apples are on the tree.
5	Look! A farmer!	e	The goats are black.

4 What Do You Eat?

Lesson 1

1 Circle.

1  fruit / sandwich

2  vegetables / want

3  lunch box / sandwich

4  sandwich / orange

5  want / vegetables

6  lunch box / orange

2 Write.

orange vegetables ~~lunch box~~ fruit want sandwich

My mum makes my lunch. I have a red
(1) lunch box. Look! Today, there is a
(2) ____________ with cheese and
(3) ____________ in it. There is an apple and an
(4) ____________, too. I really like (5) ____________!
I (6) ____________ to have my lunch, now!

3 Circle.

1 Have we got **some / any** sandwiches?

2 There are **some / any** tables, but there aren't **some / any** chairs!

3 Is there **some / any** fruit? No, but there are **some / any** vegetables.

4 Are there **some / any** toys in the toy box?

5 There are **some / any** oranges in the fridge.

6 This farm has got **some / any** beautiful fields!

4 Write *some* or *any*.

1 Are there ___any___ oranges on the table?
Yes, there are ___some___ oranges on the table.

2 Has she got ______________ brothers or sisters?
No, she hasn't got ______________ brothers or sisters.

3 Are there ______________ books on the bookshelf?
No, there aren't ______________ books on the bookshelf.

4 Have they got ______________ animals on their farm?
Yes, they've got ______________ animals on their farm.

5 Do you want ______________ fruit for breakfast?
Yes, I want ______________ fruit for breakfast.

6 Is there ______________ water in the fridge?
No, there isn't ______________ water in the fridge.

5 Draw, write and say.

This is my lunch box.

There is ______________.

There's ______________.

There are ______________.

There aren't ______________.

Lesson 2

1 Write.

20 — t w e n ty

30 — t _ _ _ _ y

40 — f _ _ _ y

50 — f _ f _ _

60 — s _ _ t _

70 — s _ _ _ _ ty

80 — e _ _ _ t _

90 — n _ _ _ _ y

100 — o _ _ h _ _ d _ _ _

2 Match.

1

2

year

piece

sugar

week

3
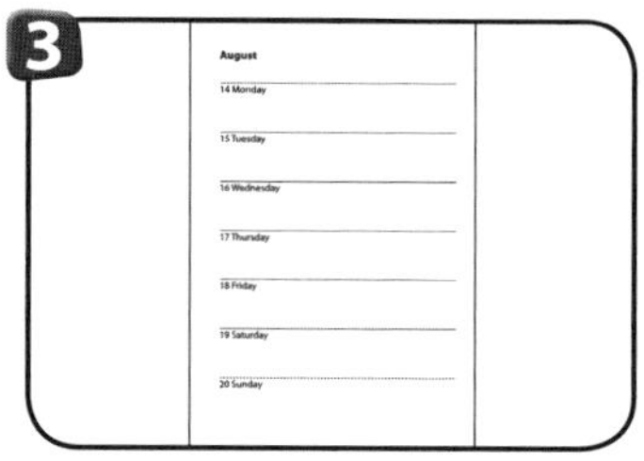

4
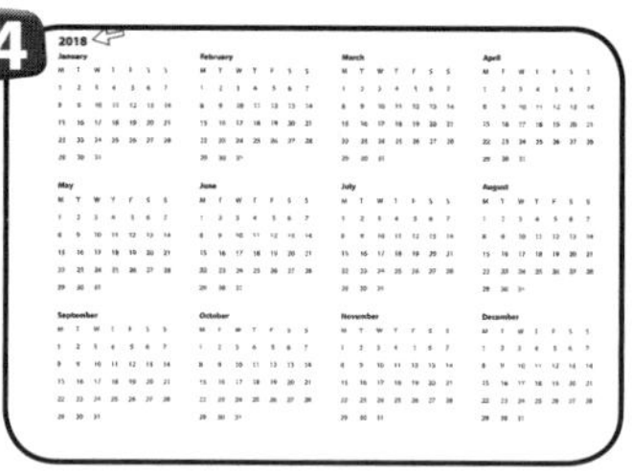

3 Circle.

1 **How much** / **How many** days are there in a week?

2 How many **pieces** / **years** of pizza are there?

3 **How much** / **How many** juice is there in the fridge?

4 **How much** / **How many** weeks are there in a year?

5 There are 52 **weeks** / **days** in a year.

6 **How much** / **How many** sandwiches are in your lunch box?

4 Write.

chicken orange sweet week ice cream chocolate ~~door~~ sugar

1 

How many doors
are there?

2 

____
______________ can we buy?

3 

____
______________ do you want?

4 

____
______________ have they got?

5 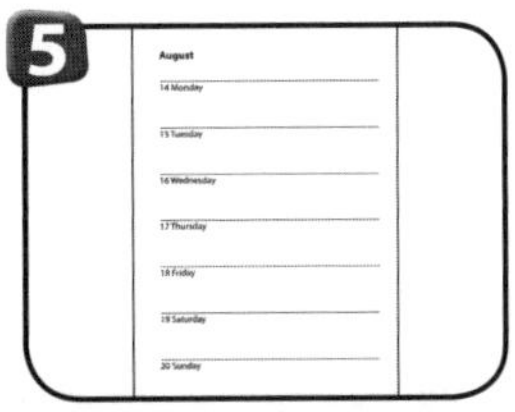

____
______________ are there?

6 

____
______________ is there?

7 

____
______________ are there?

8 

____
______________ can I have?

5 Choose and colour. Write and say.

~~black~~ blue brown green orange pink purple red white yellow

10 20 30 40 50

60 70 80 90 100

1. Ten is black.
2. Twenty is ______________.
3. Thirty is ______________.
4. Forty is ______________.
5. Fifty is ______________.
6. Sixty is ______________.
7. Seventy is ______________.
8. Eighty is ______________.
9. Ninety is ______________.
10. One hundred is ______________.

Lesson 3

1 Write.

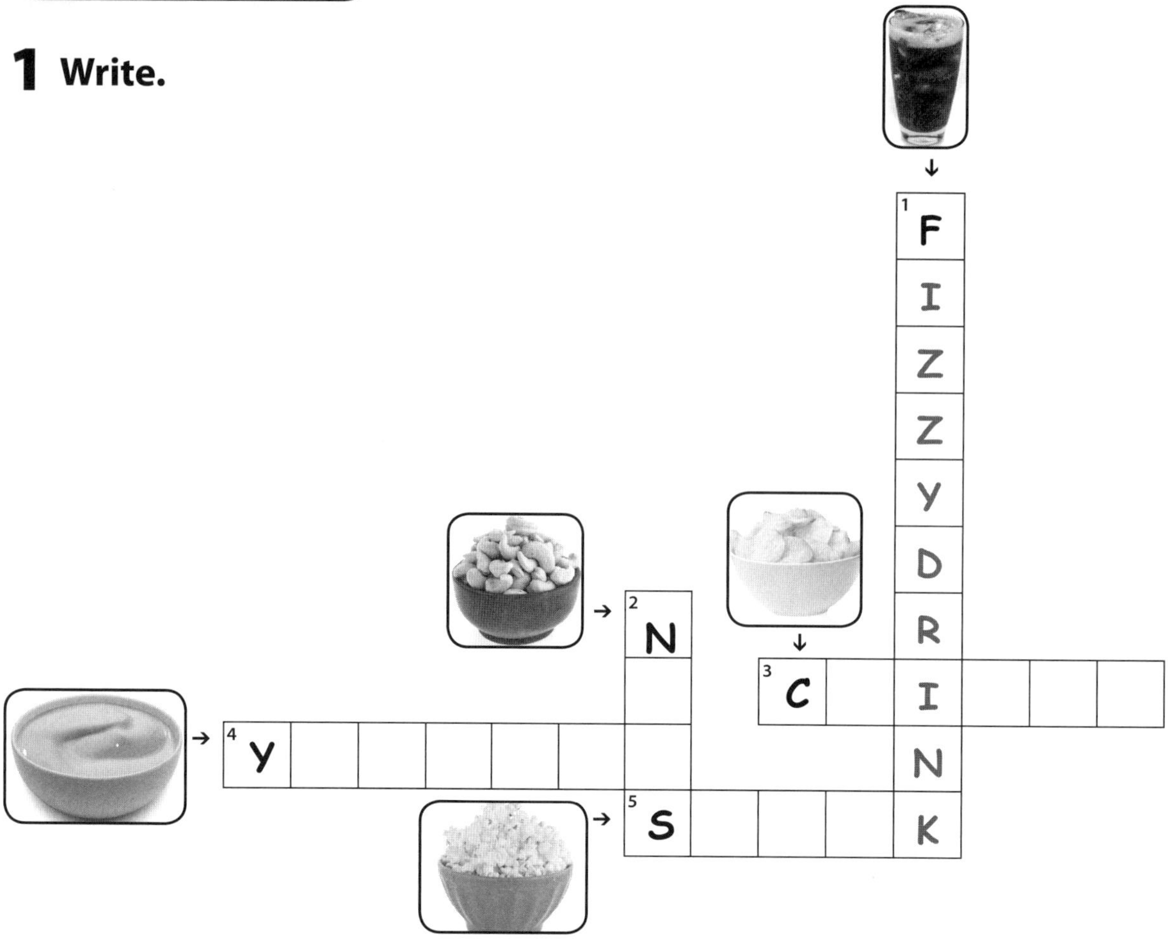

2 Read and draw.

- present to give Mum ✔
- yoghurt ✔
- crisps ✗
- fizzy drink ✔
- snack for lunch ✗
- nuts ✔

3 Write.

I	me
you	
he	
she	
it	
we	
they	

4 Write.

1 Can you feed the horses?
Can you feed them ?

2 I want to give Grandma a present.
I want to give ______ a present.

3 Look at the goat!
Look at ______ !

4 Let's make Mark and Tim some sandwiches.
Let's make ______ some sandwiches.

5 Don't throw the ball.
Catch ______!

6 Look at me and Steve.
Look at ______ .

5 Match and say.

1 I'm hungry. Can I have some fruit?

2 It's Martha's birthday!

3 I have a new computer!

4 Lisa and Kelly are really nice girls.

5 Do you want some lunch?

a Wow! Can I see it?

b Yes, you can. I've got some apples and oranges.

c Yes, they are. I like them.

d Let's give her a nice present!

e Yes, please! Can you make me a snack?

Review 2 Units 3–4

1 Write.

1 bananas
2 ______
3 ______
4 ______
5 ______
6 ______
7 ______
8 ______
9 ______
10 ______
11 ______
12 ______
13 ______
14 ______

2 Circle.

1 **There's** / **There are** 40 cows in the field.
2 Do you want **a** / **an** slice of pizza?
3 Is there **an** / **the** orange in the fridge?
4 **Is there** / **Are there** any nuts?
5 They are on **the** / **a** stairs.
6 Where is **the** / **an** door?

3 Order and write.

1 is / lunch box / whose / this / ? Whose lunch box is this?

2 give / let's / a / present / him ______________________

3 nice / this / coat / a / is ______________________

4 let's / chocolate / some / them / buy ______________________

5 farm / my / big / uncle's / is ______________________

6 bookshelf / this / whose / is / ? ______________________

4 Circle.

1 How **many** / **much** books are there on the bookshelf?

2 Are there **any** / **some** nice animals on the farm?

3 How **many** / **much** sugar do you want on your fruit?

4 There are **any** / **some** oranges in the fridge.

5 Are there **any** / **some** nuts on the table?

5 Read and draw.

What's in your lunch box?

5 What's it Like Outside?

Lesson 1

1 Circle.

1 cloud / moon

2 snow / sky

3 moon / sun

4 cloud / windy

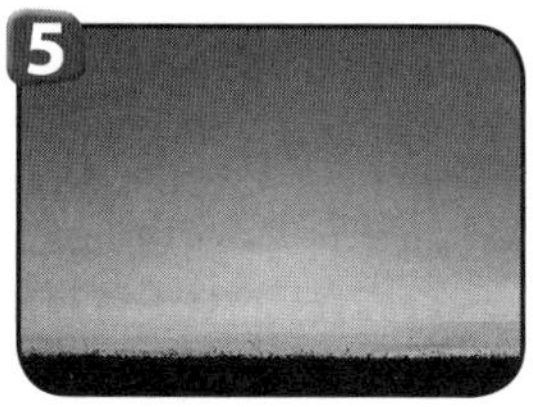

5 snow / sky

6 sun / windy

2 Write.

1 Look at the ___snow___!

2 Look, there are some ______________!

3 Look at the ______________!

4 Look at the tree. It's very ______________.

5 Look at the ______________. It's pretty.

6 There's the ______________!

3 Circle.

1 I **'re** / **'m** watering the plants.

2 Grandma **'s** / **'m** looking at the moon.

3 They **'m** / **'re** feeding the chickens.

4 Mum **'s** / **'re** having a snack.

5 Ssh! We **'s** / **'re** sleeping!

6 You **'s** / **'re** working on Saturday.

4 Write.

1 

We 're having (have) a fizzy drink.

2 

The cat ________ (sleep) on the bed.

3 

The twins ________ (play) football in the sun.

4 

It ________ (snow).

5 

The cows ________ (run).

6 

Mum ________ (listen) to music.

5 Match and say.

1 

Martin

2 

____

3 

____

4 

____

5 

____

6 

____

1 Martin's doing his homework.
2 Afrif's listening to music.
3 Jane's having a snack.
4 Tom and Mike are playing in the snow.
5 Jim and Ana are feeding the goats.
6 Yara's planting a tree.

Lesson 2

1 Write.

1. Jan u a r y
2. Fe ___ ary
3. M ___
4. ___ ril
5. ___ a ___
6. J ___
7. ___ y
8. A ___ st
9. S ___ t ___
10. ___ ber
11. Nov ___
12. D ___ r

2 Read and colour.

Autumn

___

Winter

___

Spring

___

Summer

___

3 Circle.

1 Pablo **isn't** / **aren't** going to school this month.

2 I **'m not** / **aren't** sleeping.

3 There **aren't** / **isn't** any snow.

4 We **isn't** / **aren't** eating oranges.

5 You **isn't** / **aren't** working in March.

6 The birds **isn't** / **aren't** in the sky.

4 Order and write.

1 eating / Lucy / isn't / yoghurt / her

Lucy isn't eating her yoghurt.

2 doing / not / homework / I'm / weekend / this / my

____

3 snowing / isn't / it /

____

4 dog / its / biscuits / the / eating / isn't

____

5 aren't / tennis / they / playing / this / month

____

6 park / you / going / aren't / to / the

____

5 Read, draw and say.

What's your favourite month?

Lesson 3

1 Circle.

1 

play video games / study

2 

think / watch a film

3 

stay at home / think

4 

feed the cows / watch a film

5 

study / stay at home

2 Write.

~~watch a film~~ study think staying at home play video games

1 I'm going to the cinema. I want to watch a film.
2 It's cold outside. Do you want to ______ on the computer?
3 I can't play football today. I'm ______ with my mum and dad.
4 James likes to ______. He's a good student.
5 I don't play sport. I like to read books and ______.

3 Match.

1 Are you having lunch?
2 Is your dad sleeping?
3 Is your mum reading her book?
4 Are the children studying?
5 Are you staying at home this weekend?
6 Are Andy and Kate watching a film?

a Yes, they are. They're good students!
b Yes, he is. He's tired.
c No, we aren't. We're having a snack.
d Yes, we are. We're not going to the farm.
e No, she isn't. She's sleeping.
f No, they aren't. They're watching TV.

4 Write.

1 Are they sleeping (sleep)?
No, they aren't.

2 ________ you ________ (play) video games? ________

3 ________ John ________ (play) tennis?
____

4 ________ they ________ (studying)?
No, they aren't.

5 ________ Alice ________ (think)?
____

6 ________ Tom and Ana ________ (ride) horses? ________

5 Match and say.

1 What are you doing?
2 What is Mum doing?
3 What are the children doing?
4 What is Dad doing?
5 What is the dog doing?

a She's having a fizzy drink.
b It's swimming in the river.
c They're playing video games.
d I'm thinking.
e He's making sandwiches.

6 Let's Go!

Lesson 1

1 Match.

1 

2 

3 

ski
snowboard
mountain
ice-skate
play ice hockey

4 

5 

2 Look. Tick or cross.

1 There are five people skiing. ✗
2 A dog is snowboarding. ☐
3 Two boys are ice-skating. ☐
4 There are three mountains. ☐
5 Two people are playing ice hockey. ☐

3 Match.

1 John can't watch a film. — a
2 I can see the mountains!
3 We can't go to the farm.
4 Lara can ice-skate.
5 I can't ski!

a He's playing ice hockey.
b But she can't snowboard.
c There isn't any snow.
d It's too far!
e They're really big!

4 Write.

1 Can Hilda ski (ski)?
Yes, ________.

2 ________ we ________ (go) to the mountains?
No, ________.

3 ________ Emily ________ (play) ice hockey?
No, ________.

4 ________ they ________ (water) the plants?
Yes, ________.

5 ________ Victor ________ (snowboard)?
Yes, ________.

6 ________ Jenny ________ (catch) a ball?
Yes, ________.

5 Write about you. Then say.

1 speak English ________ I can speak English.
2 play the guitar ________
3 swim ________
4 ski ________
5 catch a ball ________
6 ice-skate ________

Lesson 2

1 Circle.

1 tent / sleeping bag

3 forget / fire

5 tent / forget

7 camping / bring

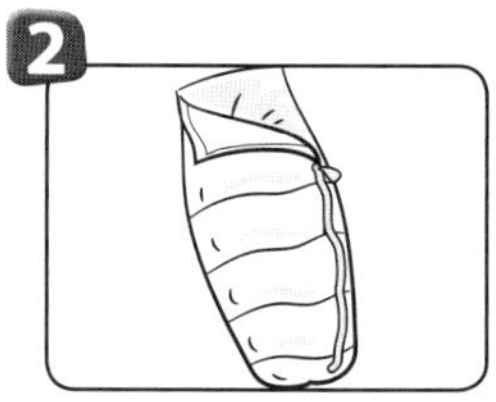

2 sleeping bag / forget

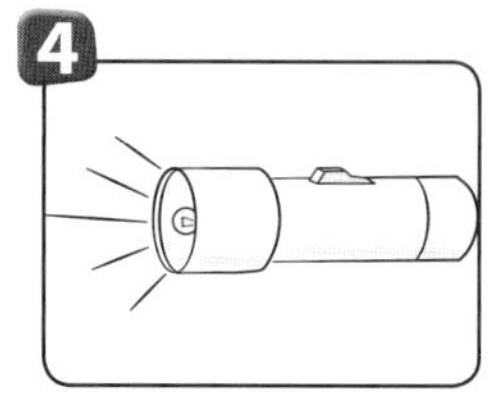

4 fire / torch

6 camping / bring sandwiches

2 Write.

tent ~~camping~~ forget bring sleeping bags fire

My family loves (1) camping. We have a green (2) ________. In the day, we walk in the fields. We (3) ________ lots of food to eat. We have sandwiches for lunch. At night, we cook dinner on the (4) ________. We sleep in (5) ____________. We mustn't (6) ________ to take a torch. It helps us to see at night.

3 Write *must* or *mustn't*.

1 You mustn't eat in the classroom.

2 You ______ listen to your teacher.

3 You ______ throw pencils.

4 You ______ draw on your desk.

5 You ______ do your homework.

6 You ______ be good.

4 Match.

1 We mustn't talk to our friends,
2 We must wear warm coats,
3 We mustn't throw the ball,
4 We mustn't run,
5 We can't watch TV,

a it's snowing today!
b we must walk.
c we must listen to our teacher.
d we must study.
e we must kick it!

5 Write and sing.

~~camping~~ torches camping camping sleeping bags mustn't tents

Let's camp in the mountains.
Let's camp by the sea.

Camping is fun for everyone, my family and me!

We're ______ tonight and we ______ forget what we need.

We've got ______ and ______, ______ and maps!

We've got what we need, my family and me!

Let's camp in the mountains.
Let's camp by the sea.

______ is fun for everyone,
my family and me!

Lesson 3

1 Write.

~~have a picnic~~ beach go hiking ride a bike forest

1 

have a picnic

3 

5 

2 

4 

2 Circle.

1 Let's make sandwiches and **have a picnic** / **play video games**.
2 I don't want to study. I want to go to the **farm** / **beach** and swim.
3 I **ride a bike** / **go hiking** to school in the summer.
4 Let's **go hiking** / **have a picnic**. We can walk in the mountains.
5 We see monkeys in the **forest** / **beach**. They live in trees.

3 Match.

1 Don't sing!	a It's really good.
2 Don't throw your book!	b It's got nice dolls.
3 Watch the film.	c They're very hungry!
4 Let's go to the park.	d This is a library.
5 Feed the horses.	e We can play football.
6 Let's look in the toy shop.	f Our teacher doesn't like it.

4 Write.

1 Sleep in a sleeping bag. Don't sleep on the floor.
2 Don't go to the mountains. ______ to the beach.
3 Write in your notebook. ______ on the wall!
4 Play football with me. ______ video games.
5 Don't sit on your desk. ______ on your chair.
6 Throw the ball. ______ the sandwich!

5 Write and say.

1

3

5

2

4

6

1 Let's go camping this weekend.
2 ______ this summer.
3 ______ in the mountains on Sunday.
4 ______ on the beach.
5 ______ in the forest.
6 ______ in the park.

Review 3 Units 5–6

1 Write.

snowboard cloud ~~sun~~ mountain ski ice-skate
snow beach October ice hockey August
March home windy May forest

Outside	Sports	Months	Places
sun			

2 Match.

1 

2 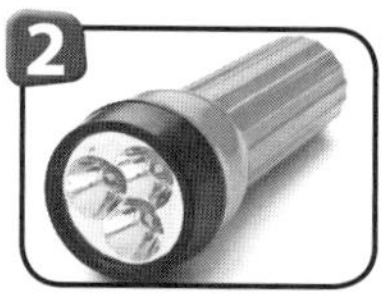

3 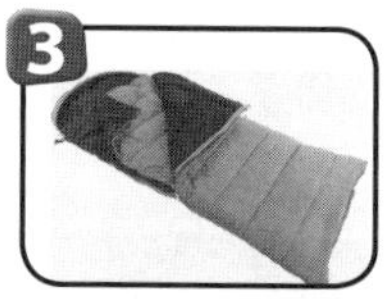

4 

5 

6 

7 

8 

a sleeping bag

b go hiking

c have a picnic

d ride a bike

e fire

f tent

g torch

h go camping

3 Write

1 We ___'re playing___ (play) video games!

2 ________________ (she / study)? Yes, she is.

3 He ________________ (not / watch) a film now.

4 I ________________ (throw) the ball!

5 ________________ (they / stay) at home? No, they aren't.

6 You ________________ (not / think) about sleeping, are you?

4 Circle.

✗ ✓ ✗ ✗ ✓ ✓

1 You **must** / **(mustn't)** talk in the library.

2 You **must** / **mustn't** study.

3 You **must** / **mustn't** ride a bike in the park.

4 You **must** / **mustn't** eat in the car.

5 You **must** / **mustn't** feed the cat this weekend.

6 You **must** / **mustn't** bring your torch.

5 Read and draw. Say.

What do you like outside?

7 Jobs

Lesson 1

1 Match.

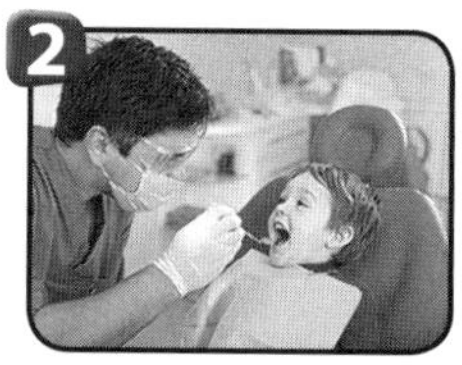

cook
postman
dentist
doctor
photographer

2 Write.

dentist doctor cook ~~postwoman~~ photographer

1 Our postwoman comes every morning.
2 The ______________ makes really good pizzas!
3 This ______________ likes to take photos of forests.
4 Can I see the ______________ ? My teeth aren't good.
5 Help! Is there a ______________ here?

3 Write.

1 Penny watches (watch) DVDs on Saturday.
2 Tim ______________ (play) with his cousins on Sunday.
3 Emma ______________ (go) to the library on Tuesday.
4 The postman ______________ (ride) his bike every day.
5 Mum ______________ (study) English at night.
6 Mr and Mrs Brown ______________ (read) lots of books.

4 Circle.

1 

They **study** / **studies** at school.

2 

John **eat** / **eats** biscuits every weekend!

3 

Mary **play** / **plays** the piano in the afternoon.

4 

We **go** / **goes** to the beach in summer.

5 

The cat **sleep** / **sleeps** on my bed every night.

6 

Anne **read** / **reads** books on Saturdays.

5 Write about you. Say.

1 I play the guitar on Mondays.

2 I ________________ on Wednesdays.

3 I ________________ on Fridays.

4 I ________________ on Saturdays.

5 I ________________ on Sundays.

Lesson 2

1 Write.

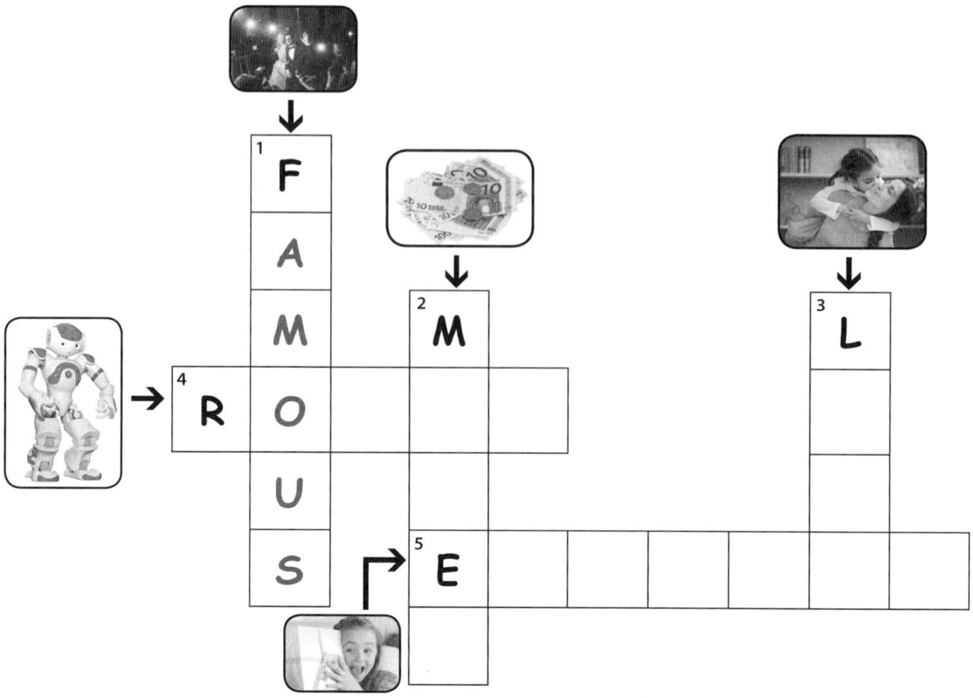

2 Circle.

1 How much **money / robots** do you have? I want to buy this tent.

2 I'm very **excited / unusual** about seeing this film. It's about doctors.

3 Danny makes **horses / robots** that can swim. They take photographs of fish.

4 Anne is a **famous / excited** photographer. Her photos are in the museum.

5 James is an **unusual / tired** dentist. He works with elephants' teeth!

6 I **watch / love** my job. I'm happy.

3 Match.

1 It's Saturday!

2 Mary likes fruit.

3 Pete plays the guitar.

4 The doctor is tired.

5 I'm not thirsty.

a She doesn't like biscuits.

b She doesn't sleep at night.

c I don't want a fizzy drink.

d We don't have school!

e He doesn't play the drums.

4 Circle *don't* or *doesn't*.

1 Simon **don't** / **doesn't** watch TV in the morning.

2 They **don't** / **doesn't** eat crisps every day.

3 I **don't** / **doesn't** like skiing.

4 Grandma **don't** / **doesn't** go to school.

5 We **don't** / **doesn't** study on Mondays.

6 Uncle Paul **don't** / **doesn't** have a robot.

7 You **don't** / **doesn't** ride your bike to school.

8 Penny **don't** / **doesn't** read every night.

5 Write and sing.

famous	~~unusual~~	hockey players	unusual
unusual	unusual	money	robot makers

Let's do something ___unusual___.
Let's do something fun!
Do we work just for ______________?
No, we don't!
Do we work to be ______________?
No, we don't!
We want to do something ______________.
We want to do something fun!
Let's do something ______________.
Let's do something fun!
Can we be ______________?
Yes, we can!
Can we be ______________?
Yes, we can!
We want to do something ______________.
We want to do something fun!

Lesson 3

1 Write.

pilot actor ~~nurse~~ vet astronaut firefighter

1

He helps people: nurse

2

He's on TV: ______

3

She walks on the moon: ______

4
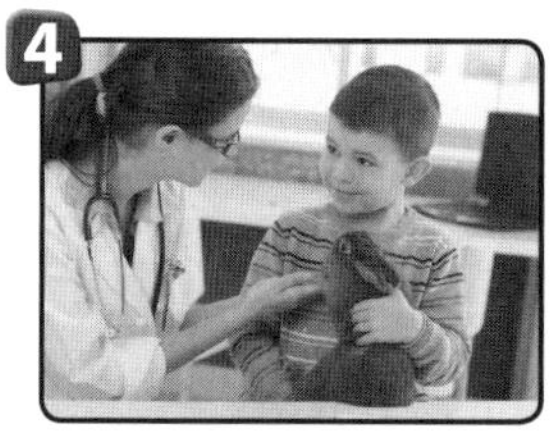

She helps animals: ______

5

He flies an aeroplane: ______

6

He helps with fires: ______

2 Circle.

1 **Do** / **Does** she love her job?
Yes, she **do** / **does**.

2 **Do** / **Does** you go to school in the morning?
Yes, we **do / does**.

3 **Do** / **Does** they work at the weekend?
No, they **don't / doesn't**.

4 **Do** / **Does** Mike work with animals?
Yes, he **do / does**.

5 **Do** / **Does** Susan have any money?
No, she **don't / doesn't**.

3 Match.

~~pilot~~ nurse astronaut vet actor firefighter

1 pilot
2 ______
3 ______
4 ______
5 ______
6 ______

4 Read and tick.

				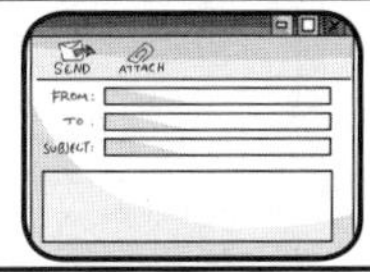
Omar 	✔	✔	✔	✘
Anna 	✘	✔	✘	✘

1 Does Omar like fizzy drinks?
Yes, he does.

2 Does Anna speak French?
______

3 Do Anna and Omar play sports?
______

4 Does Omar speak French?
______

5 Does Anna like fizzy drinks?
______

6 Do Anna and Omar like email?
______

5 Write about you.

1 Do you like school? Yes, I do.

2 Does your friend like fizzy drinks? ______

3 Do you ride a bike? ______

4 Do your family like to go hiking? ______

5 Do you play sports? ______

6 Do you have a pet? ______

8 Technology

Lesson 1

1 Match.

1 

2 

3 

4 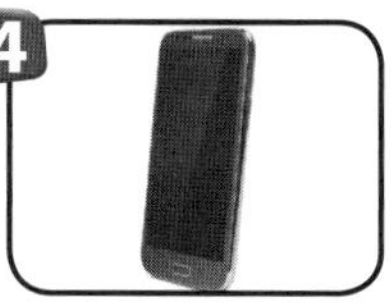

5 

6 

a screen

b email

c answer

d tablet

e keyboard

f phone

2 Write.

1 We want this when we have a question. a n s w e r

2 This is a small, thin computer. t _ _ _ _ _

3 You use this to write on a computer. k _ _ _ _ _ _ _

4 You can talk to your friend on this. p _ _ _ _

5 We look at pictures on this. s _ _ _ _ _

6 You write this to friends and family. e _ _ _ _

3 Order and write.

1 night / book / reads / Dad / a / sometimes / at

Dad sometimes reads a book at night.

2 it / in / August / warm / always / is

____

3 school / never / I / emails / at / write

____

4 January / often / is / in / cold / it

____

4 Read and colour.

always = red   sometimes = blue   never = green   often = yellow

1
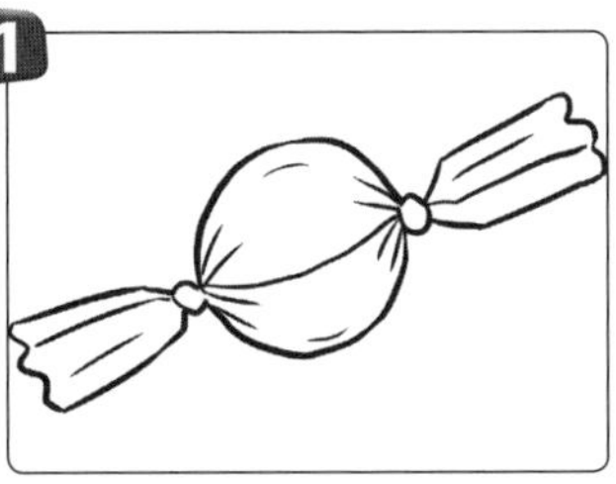

2

3
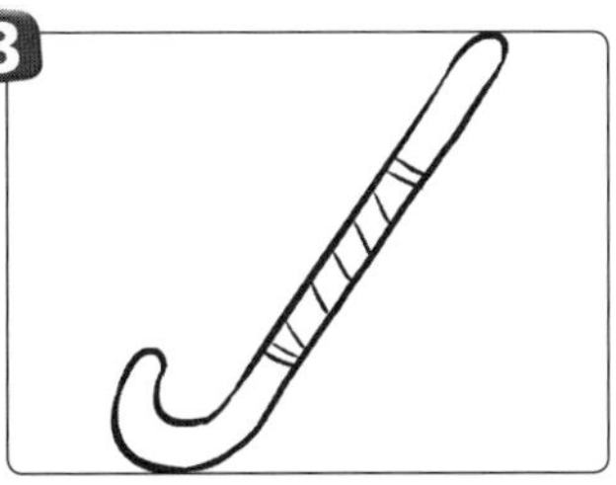

4

5

6

Jane never eats sweets. She often eats fruit. She loves ice hockey and she sometimes plays it on Saturdays. Jane often talks to her grandma on the phone. Her desk is never messy and she always does her homework.

5 Write about you.

1 do homework ______ I always do my homework.

2 go to the cinema ______________________

3 swim in the sea ______________________

4 write emails ______________________

Lesson 2

1 Circle.

1 

easy / app

4 

quick / slow

2 

easy / slow

5 

busy / app

3 

busy / difficult

6 

slow / difficult

2 Circle.

1 Sometimes my school lessons are **difficult / quick**.
2 I can't watch TV. I'm really **busy / app**.
3 Do you have this new **app / cow** on your phone?
4 Elephants are **slow / easy** animals.
5 My homework is **easy / slow**. Mum isn't helping me.
6 Ice hockey players are very **busy / quick**.

3 Match.

1 Summer is
2 Skiing is
3 The green birds are
4 The boy is
5 Tractors are

a happier than the girl.
b smaller than the red birds.
c better than snowboarding.
d slower than cars.
e warmer than winter.

4 Order and write.

1 is / Vicky / than / shorter / Sissy Sissy is shorter than Vicky.

2 Dan / Bill / is / than / taller ____________________

3 happier / is / Vicky /Sissy / than ____________________

4 than / longer / Sissy / hair / got / May / has

____

5 Write and say.

easier (x2) app emails ~~better~~ quicker (x2) better (x3)

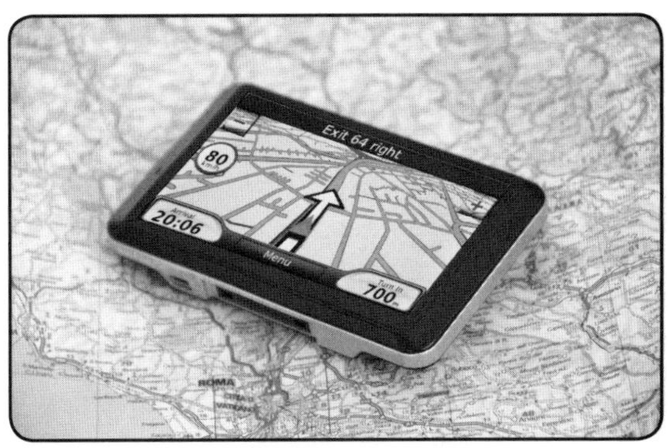

What's better than a letter?
An email!
It's __________. It's __________.
Oh, an email is __________ than a letter.

What's __________ than a map?
An app!
It's __________. It's __________.
Oh, an app is __________ than a map.

Technology can really help us.
It can help both me and you!
A smartphone __________, for __________ or maps …
There's always something that's brand new.

Lesson 3

1 Match.

1
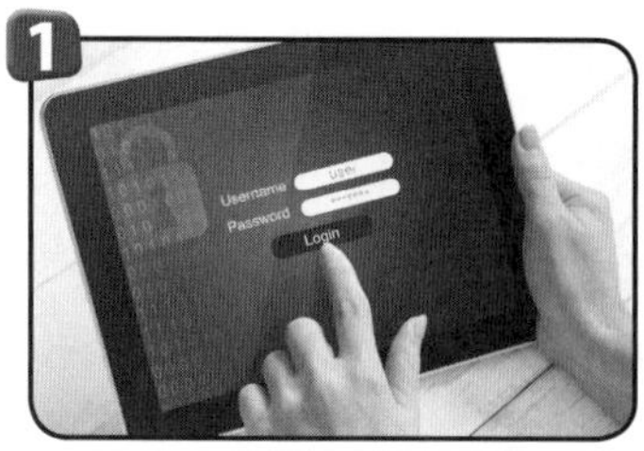

a share

2

b password

3

c safe

4
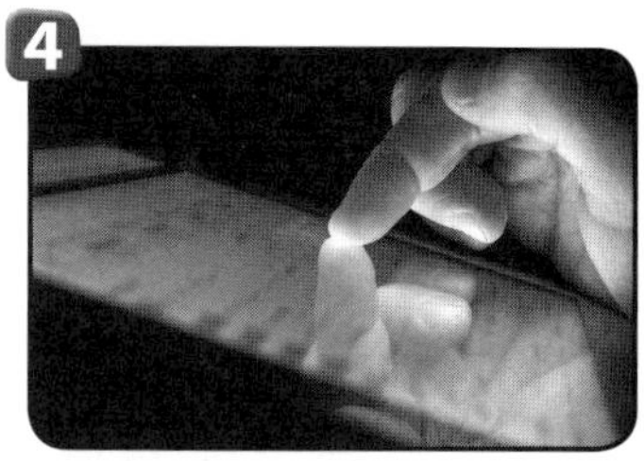

d touch

5

e send

2 Circle.

1 Passwords help you to stay **safe / send** on a computer.

2 Use your hand to **share / touch** the screen.

3 Can you **touch / send** an email to your cousin?

4 Don't forget your **share / password**!

5 Can you **touch / share** your photographs with me?

6 English is difficult! Do you **need / share** any help?

3 Circle.

1 John is the **tallest** / **taller** child in the family.

2 This is the **nicer / nicest** beach.

3 This is the **biggest / big** whale in the water.

4 My mum is the **busier / busiest** woman in the world.

5 Rex is the **worst / bad** dog on the farm.

6 Pizzas are the **better / best** food.

4 Write.

1

My new app is the ________ (good) one on my phone.

2

Your desk is the ________ (tidy) desk at school.

3

Ben and Bob are the ________ (cute) rabbits.

4

This tablet is the ________ (quick) in the shop.

5

It's the ________ (safe) car you can buy.

5 Read and draw. Say.

This is a giraffe.
It's the tallest animal.
I think it's the best animal!

Review 4 Units 7–8

1 Find, circle and write.

D	K	B	A	U	D	A	P	P	W
E	M	A	I	L	O	H	W	S	A
N	F	S	T	P	C	K	I	H	C
T	P	I	L	O	T	E	V	E	T
I	A	O	O	L	O	Y	D	S	O
S	R	W	N	O	R	B	Y	C	R
T	A	B	L	E	T	O	I	R	N
C	L	O	U	D	Y	A	M	E	K
P	A	S	S	W	O	R	D	E	H
C	O	O	K	C	F	D	X	N	Q

Jobs

cook
____
____
____
____
____

Computers

app
____
____
____
____
____

2 Write.

1 Do you like oranges? No, I don't .

2 Does he want a chocolate? Yes, __________ .

3 __________ you play ice hockey in the winter? No, __________.

4 __________ your grandma watch TV? Yes, __________ .

5 __________ they work at the weekend? No, they __________ .

3 Match.

1	My aunt's an astronaut.	a	She often flies near the moon!
2	I want to see your photos.	b	Can you answer it, please?
3	I have a question.	c	Can you share them with me?
4	Firefighters have a difficult job.	d	Yes, you do. You always need to be safe.
5	I want to be a nurse.	e	They always help people in fires.
6	Do you want to be famous?	f	I love to help people.
7	Do I need an unusual password?	g	No, I don't! I don't need lots of money.

4 Circle.

1 Can you send me the **best** / **good** photo?

2 She's the **cleverer** / **cleverest** photographer I know.

3 The tablet is **fastest** / **faster** than the computer.

4 The robot is **quicker** / **quickest** than a postman.

5 Ice hockey is **safest** / **safer** than skiing.

6 Football is the **easiest** / **easy** sport.

5 Write about you.

I always ______________________

I sometimes ______________________

I often ______________________

I never ______________________

9 Before Our Time

Lesson 1

1 Match.

1 
2 
3 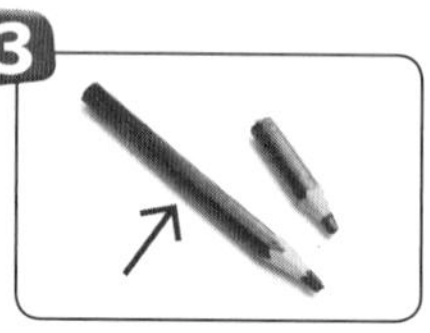
4 
5 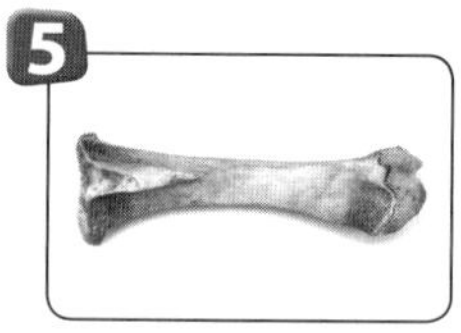

a long **b** hunt **c** dinosaur **d** fossil **e** bone

2 Read and colour.

1 Look at the fossils. The biggest fossil is black.

2 Look at the dinosaurs. The smallest dinosaur is green.

3 Look at the bones. The longest bone is brown.

4 The boy is looking for fossils. His trousers are red and his T-shirt is blue.

5 The history book is yellow.

3 Circle.

1 I was / were at the beach yesterday.

2 The dinosaur museum **was** / **were** fun!

3 We **was** / **were** excited to see the shark's bone.

4 The red dinosaur **was** / **were** very big.

5 Johnny and Kate **was** / **were** at a history lesson.

6 Jackie **was** / **were** tired last night.

4 Write.

It was He was She was They were ~~You were~~ We were

You were at the farm.

__________ my first piano lesson yesterday.

__________ very tired.

__________ at the park on Sunday.

__________ at the museum yesterday.

__________ on the tractor.

5 Write and say.

We're exc_i_ted to learn about b_g d_nosaurs _n our h_story lesson.

Lesson 2

1 Write.

~~afraid~~ plant friendly Earth lizard sharp

1 

afraid

3 

______

5 

______

2 

______

4 

______

6 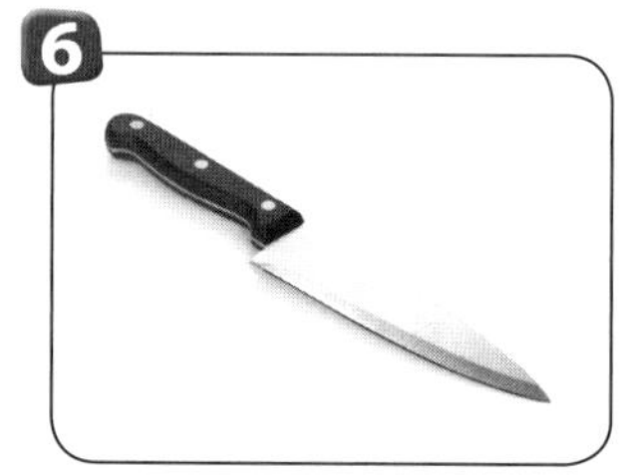

______

2 Match.

friendly ~~plant~~ lizard Earth sharp afraid

1 We got Grandma a plant for her birthday.
2 There was a small, green ______ in the garden.
3 Its teeth were very ______.
4 I was ______ of spiders.
5 There are lots of amazing animals on ______.
6 Those kids are very ______.

3 Circle.

1 Mum (**wasn't**)/ **weren't** at home on Friday.
2 There **wasn't** / **weren't** a library near the house.
3 The children **wasn't** / **weren't** afraid of the dinosaur.
4 It **wasn't** / **weren't** a big fossil.
5 Pam **wasn't** / **weren't** at school today.
6 The firefighters **wasn't** / **weren't** very happy.

4 Circle.

1

The boys **were** / **weren't** at a museum.
They **were** / **weren't** in the forest.

2

They **were** / **weren't** at the park.
They **were** / **weren't** on the mountain.

3

I **was** / **wasn't** with my friends.
I **was** / **wasn't** playing a video game.

4

Tina **was** / **wasn't** at the library.
She **was** / **wasn't** at the beach.

5

Rob and Simon **were** / **weren't** at school.
They **were** / **weren't** at a toy shop.

6

Mum and Carrie **were** / **weren't** in the garden
They **were** / **weren't** at the theatre.

5 Write and sing.

bones (x2) ~~history~~ (x2) plants short fossils (x2) meat long

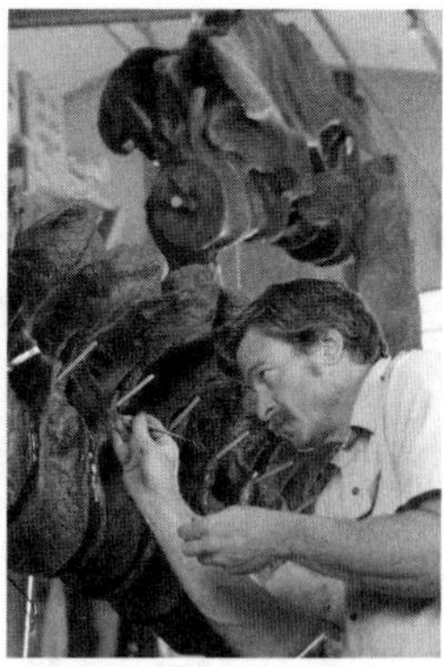

Oh, history's a mystery! There are things we'll never know. But ______ and ______ can help us, understand life from long ago!

A dinosaur bone can tell us if it was ______ or ______, if it was very clever, or if it was very strong.

A dinosaur bone can tell us, if it liked ______ or ______, if it had very big legs, or if it had little feet.

Oh, ______ a mystery! There are things we'll never know.
But ______ and ______ can help us understand life from long ago!

Lesson 3

1 Circle.

1 cave / early

3 know / dark

2 strong / cave

4 early man / long man

2 Write.

strong dark caves early know

1 Cavemen live in c a v e s.

2 It is very d _ _ _ at night.

3 Do you k _ _ _ my friend Sofia?

4 I often get up e _ _ _ _ at the weekend.

5 My dad is very s _ _ _ _ _.

3 Circle and match.

1 **Was** / **Were** it hot in the summer?

2 **Was** / **Were** he a firefighter?

3 **Was** / **Were** the bones very small?

4 **Was** / **Were** Mum at home?

5 **Was** / **Were** you at the library yesterday?

a Yes, he was.

b Yes, we were.

c No, they weren't.

d No, she wasn't.

e Yes, it was.

4 Write *was, wasn't, were* or *weren't*.

1

Were early people strong?
Yes, they were.

3

_______ the history book on the table? Yes, it _______.

2

_______ the lesson about history?
No, it _______.

4

_______ they at home yesterday? No, they _______.

5 Write and say.

1

Was Jenny at the library?
Yes, she was.

3

Were they at a museum yesterday?
_______.

2

Were they in a maths lesson?
_______.

4

Was it raining on your bike ride?
_______.

10 Cool Places

Lesson 1

1 Write.

1

building

3

____

5

____

2

____

4

____

2 Match.

1
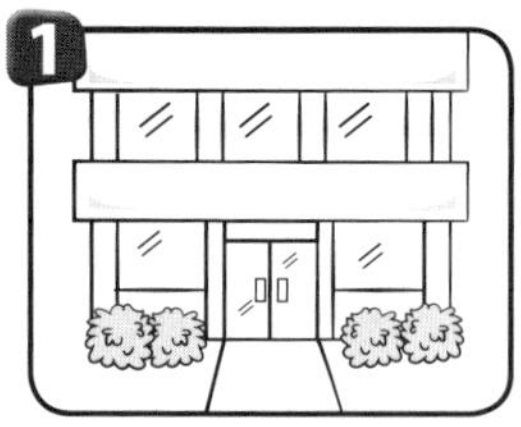

2

3

tower

castle

building

high

bridge

4
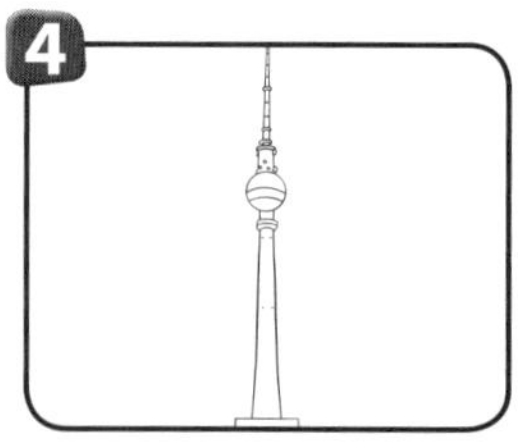

5

3 Circle.

1 My mum **cooked / climbed** this pizza. It's yummy!

2 I **play / played** video games yesterday.

3 My dog **jumped / studied** in the snow!

4 You were tired so you **stayed / stay** at home.

5 Patty **watched / listened** a film with her cousin at the weekend.

4 Write.

Last week, in my history class we (1) studied (study) castles. On Wednesday we (2) ______ (walk) to the castle in our town. We (3) ______ (watch) a film about the castle. Then we (4) ______ (climb) the stairs to the tower. It was very high but I (5) ______ (like) it! I (6) ______ (want) a photo so I used my phone. Do you like it?

5 Write and say.

1 She visited the castle.

2 ______.

3 ______.

4 ______.

5 ______.

6 ______.

Lesson 2

1 Circle.

build / desert

large / pyramid

statue / desert

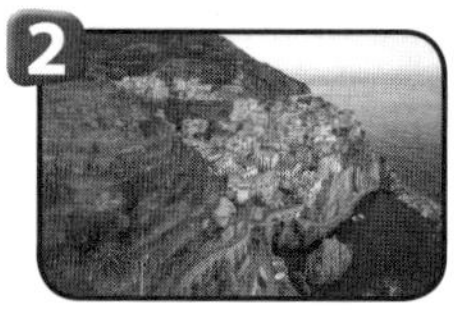

build / village

desert / statue

pyramid / large

2 Write.

build pyramid large statue ~~village~~ desert

1 The houses in our village are small.

2 Elephants are very ________ animals.

3 It's hot in the ________.

4 That ________ is very old and big.

5 There is a ________ of a famous doctor in the museum.

6 I ________ sandcastles on the beach.

3 Match.

a Camels live in the desert.

b I visited the Pyramids.

c Dad built a house in Greece.

d We saw a statue in the village.

e Our town is very busy.

f We went to the cinema last week.

4 Write.

buy build go catch have ~~eat~~

1

Bobby ___ate___ a big pizza.

2

They ________ to the Pyramids last summer.

3

We ________ a house in a village.

4

Tina ________ a new bag.

5

Tom and Paul ________ a fish by the river!

6

Yesterday, I ________ to get up at 7 o'clock.

5 Read and draw. Then say.

Last year, I went to the desert.

I saw the Pyramids and some statues.

Lesson 3

1 Write.

Brazilian Spanish American Japanese Greek
country Egyptian learn ~~travel~~

1 

travel

3 

5 

7 

9 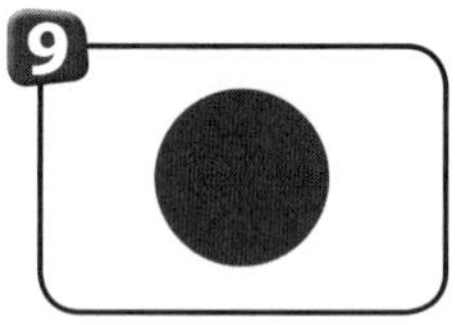

2 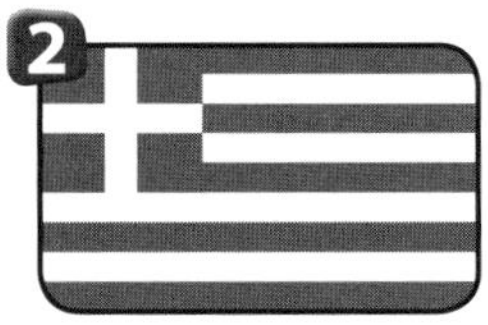

4 

6 

8 

2 Match. Then colour.

1 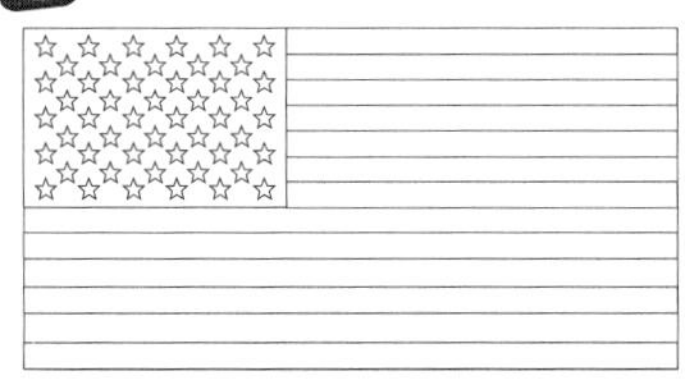

2 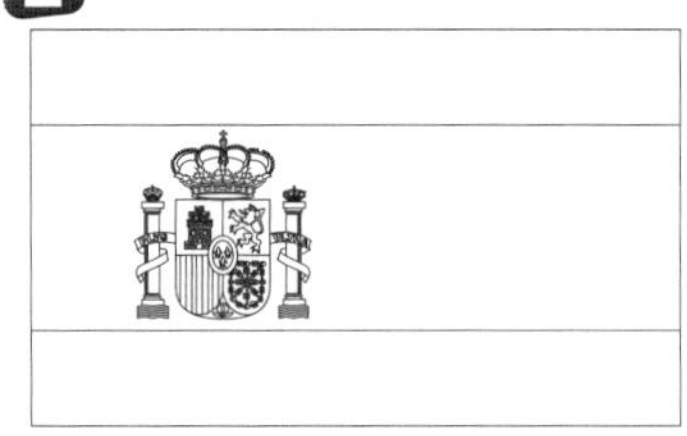

3 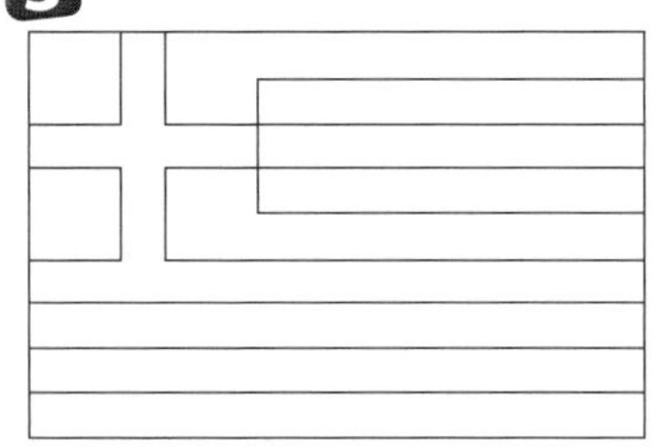

Japanese
Brazilian
American
Spanish
Greek
Egyptian

4 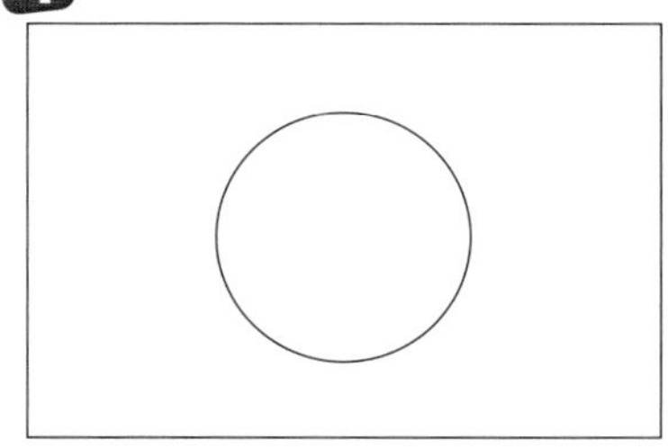

5 

6 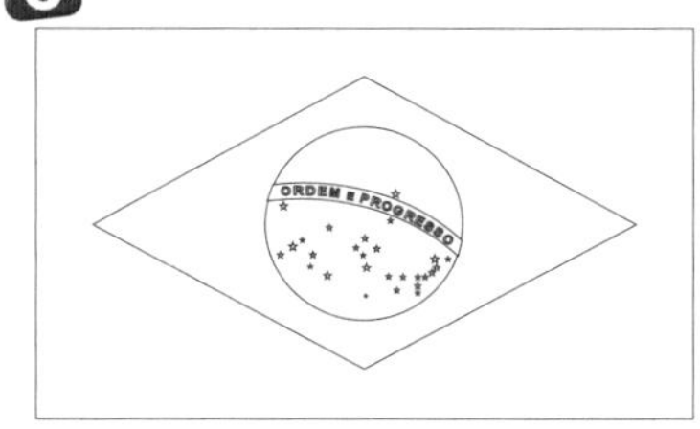

3 Circle.

1 They **didn't have** / **didn't had** a history lesson today.

2 We **didn't eat** / **didn't ate** Greek food last night.

3 They **build didn't** / **didn't build** a bridge on the river.

4 You **didn't not** / **didn't like** the dinosaur museum.

5 I **didn't caught** / **didn't catch** any fish last summer.

6 She **didn't share** / **shared** her chocolate with me.

4 Write.

1 Helena ate Japanese food. She didn't eat Spanish food.

2 Early people lived in caves. They __________ in houses.

3 Alan stayed at home. He __________ in the castle.

4 Victor caught a big fish! He __________ a small fish.

5 Asma built a gold house. She __________ a pyramid!

6 Grandpa had a Brazilian friend. He __________ an Egyptian friend.

5 Write about you. Then draw and colour.

____

____

____

____

____

Review 5 Units 9–10

1 Write.

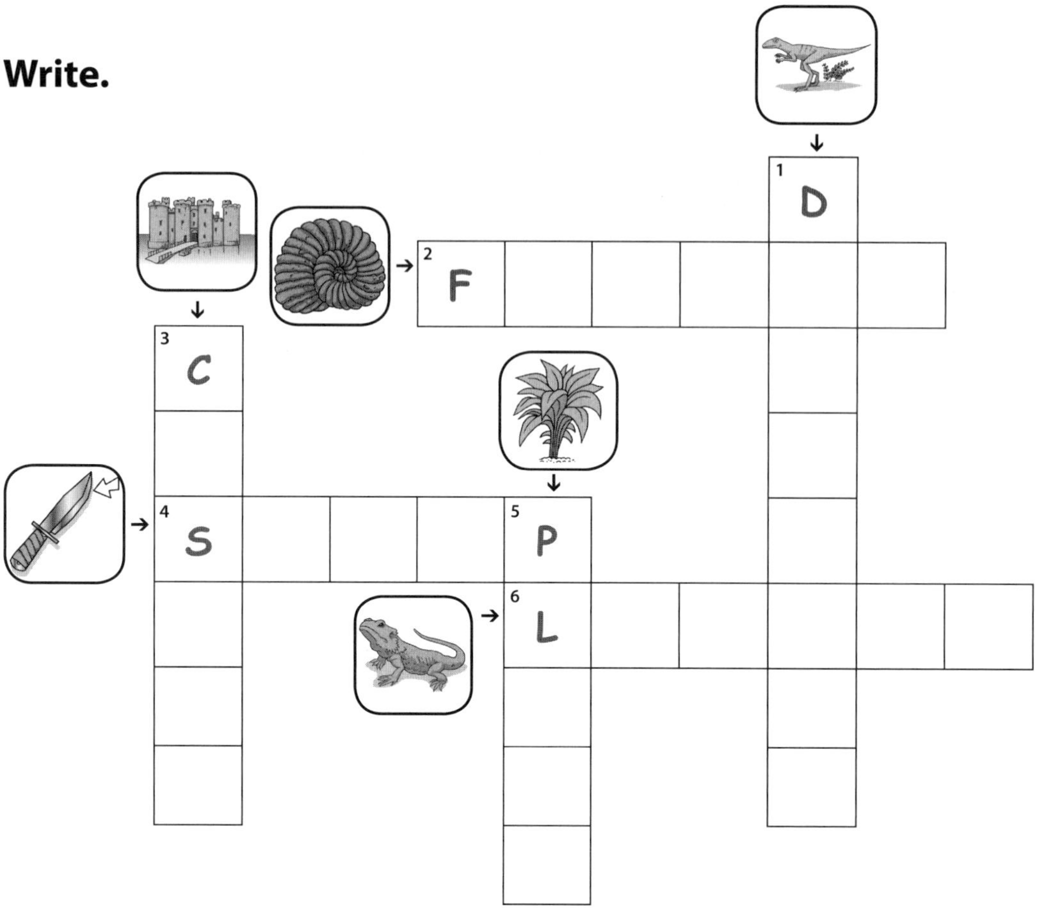

2 Match.

1 Are you studying dinosaurs at school?
2 Do you like studying history?
3 Were early people strong?
4 Did early people have nice houses?
5 Do you like Brazilian food?
6 Are they building a new bridge?

a Yes, they are.
b Yes, I am.
c No, I don't.
d Yes, I do.
e Yes, they were.
f No, they didn't.

3 Write.

1 My mum ___gave___ (give) me a diary last week.

2 I ______________ (study) for three hours yesterday.

3 Fred ______________ (not catch) a fish.

4 Sam ______________ (do) her homework this morning.

5 They ______________ (not stay) at home last weekend.

6 I ______________ (cook) lunch for you. Are you hungry?

7 ______________ (was) it cold yesterday?

4 Circle.

1

They **didn't built** / **built** a castle.

3

He **didn't live** / **lived** in a cave.

2

We **were** / **weren't** afraid of the lion.

4

The statue **was** / **wasn't** in the forest.

5 Read and write about you.

Last summer, my family went to the mountains.

We walked in the forest.

We caught some fish in the river.

We often had a picnic.

There weren't any caves.

Last summer, ______________________

____

____

____

____

____

____

____

11 Keep it Clean

Lesson 1

1 Write.

pavement fountain walk sign ~~bin~~ street town centre

1

bin

3

____

5

____

7

____

2

____

4

____

6

____

2 Write and colour.

~~girl walking~~ bin fountain pavement sign street

1 girl walking
2 __________
3 __________
4 __________
5 __________
6 __________

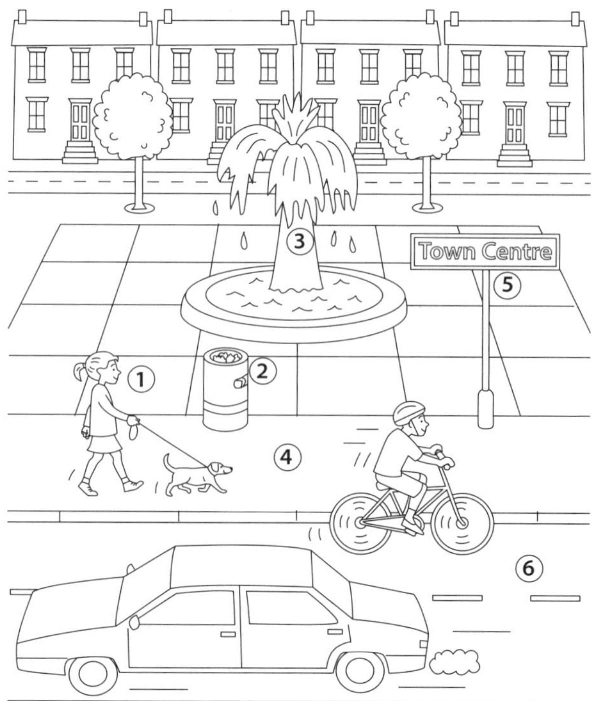

3 Circle.

1

Did you buy a bike?
Yes, I did. / No, I didn't.

2

Did Mum buy a car?
Yes, she did. / No, she didn't.

3

Did the cat eat the fish?
Yes, it did. / No, it didn't.

4

Did he catch a fish?
Yes, he did / No, he didn't.

5

Did they win the game?
Yes, they did. / No, they didn't.

6

Did you pack the map?
Yes, I did. / No, I didn't.

4 Match.

1 Did you have pizza for lunch? — a No, they didn't.
2 Did the twins do their homework? — b Yes, she did.
3 Did Mary walk on the pavement? — c Yes, it did.
4 Did the lizard sleep in the sun? — d No, I didn't.
5 Did you have a history lesson today? — e Yes, we did.
6 Did Bill play football today? — f No, he didn't.

5 Write and say.

My house is on Beach Str_ _t, betw_ _n the toy shop and café. It's n_ _r the library.

Lesson 2

1 Circle.

dirty / pick up

drop litter / clean

rubbish / drop litter

rubbish / clean

pick up / dirty

2 Match.

1 The kitchen is dirty.

2 Did you pick up the rubbish?

3 Don't drop litter in the river.

4 Please clean the table.

a Please put it in the bin!

b There's lemonade on the floor and food on the table!

c There's ice cream on it.

d It isn't good for the fish.

3 Write.

1 I am going to play football.
I'm going to play football.

2 They are going to walk to school.

____

3 He is going to help his grandma.

____

4 We are going to watch a film.

____

5 You are going to eat some vegetables!

____

4 Write.

clean watch ~~make~~ walk

1

We 're going to make
a sandwich!

2

We ________________
to the castle.

3

This room is messy!
You ________________ it.

4

It's her birthday!
She ________________ a film.

5 Write and sing.

pick it up rubbish clean (x4) bin (x2) ~~pavement~~

When you're walking on the pavement, look all around. Is ____________ all inside the ____________? Or is some on the ground?
If it's on the ground, you know what to do! Just ____________!

Keep it ____________! Keep it ____________! We want to do our part! So now, let's start! We're going to keep our town clean!

When you're riding in the car, having a snack. Don't throw the bag out of the window! Be sure to bring it back. When you take it home, you know what to do! Put it in the ____________!

Keep it ____________! Keep it ____________! We want to do our part! So now, let's start! We're going to keep our town clean!

Lesson 3

1 Match.

1
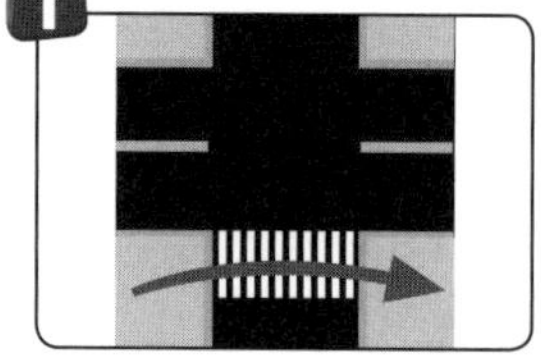

2

opposite
cross the road
turn right
turn left
go straight on

3
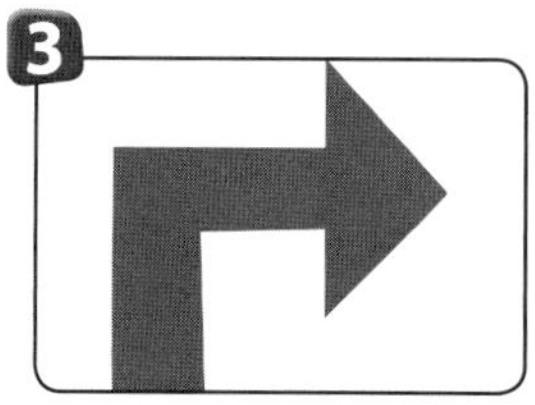

4

5

2 Write.

1

straight on

3

____

5
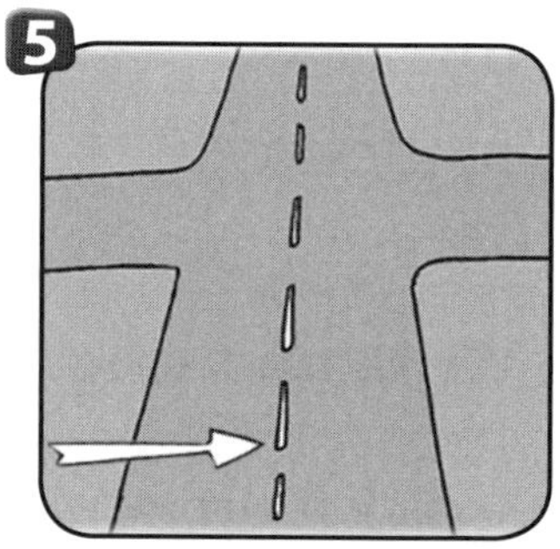

____

2

____

4
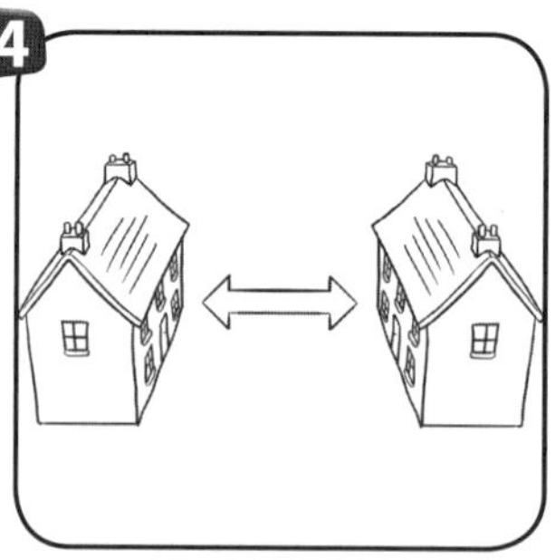

____

3 Circle.

1 I'm not going to / isn't going to have lunch now.

2 They **aren't going to** / **isn't going to** go to the beach.

3 You **aren't going to** / **'m not going to** turn left.

4 Ruby **aren't going to** / **isn't going to** cross the road.

5 It **'m not going to** / **isn't going to** snow this winter.

6 We **aren't going to** / **isn't going to** forget the map.

4 Write.

1 We aren't going to see the Pyramids!

2 Susie ______________________ buy a new phone.

3 I ______________________ share my photos.

4 You ______________________ go to school today.

5 Bill and Barry ______________________ build a castle.

6 Dad ______________________ feed the dog.

5 Write and say.

cross left straight opposite turn ~~museum~~

How do I get to the museum ?

Go __________ on. __________ right at the library and __________ the road. Then turn __________ at the school. The museum is __________ the cinema!

12 On Holiday

Lesson 1

1 Find, circle and write.

visit journey hotel meet ~~arrive~~ leave

J	L	M	L	E	D	J	R
O	D	N	M	E	E	T	H
U	G	R	L	E	A	V	E
R	P	V	X	C	R	O	V
N	T	I	Q	O	R	W	K
E	V	S	B	M	I	V	Z
Y	P	I	E	I	V	Q	F
H	O	T	E	L	E	B	M

1 

arrive

4 

______

2 

______

5 

______

3 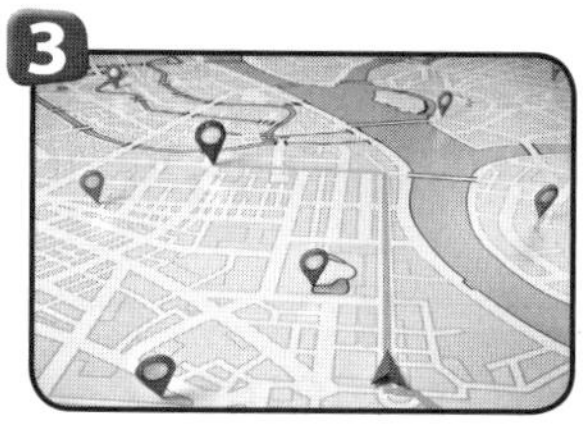

______

6 

______

2 Circle.

1 Are you going to **arrive / forget** this morning or this afternoon?

2 I'm staying at a very nice **museum / hotel** this weekend.

3 We're going to **meet / needs** our aunt at the cinema tonight.

4 It's going to be a long **dinner / journey** to the farm. It's far from our house.

5 He often **plays / visits** his son in Greece.

6 We can **see / leave** school at 2:00 today!

3 Write.

1 Is he going to stay in a hotel?
   Yes, he is. ✔
2 Am I going to clean the house?
   ________. ✔
3 Are they going to cross the road?
   ________. ✘
4 Is she going to have fish for breakfast?
   ________. ✘
5 Is it going to be a long journey?
   ________. ✔
6 Are we going to meet our friends?
   ________. ✘

4 Write.

1 Is Helen going to buy (Helen / buy) a new tablet?
2 ________ (you / go) to school?
3 ________ (Arif / play) a video game?
4 ________ (Dad / ride) his bike?
5 ________ (Amalia / have) a picnic?
6 ________ (he / stay) at home today?

5 Match and say.

1	Are Jen and Bill going to eat a pizza?	a	No, they aren't.
2	Is Paul going to do his homework?	b	Yes, it is.
3	Are the boys going to plant a tree?	c	Yes, they are.
4	Is the cat going to drink the water?	d	No, she isn't.
5	Is Julie going to draw a picture?	e	No, he isn't.

Lesson 2

1 Match.

fly

aeroplane

go sightseeing

airport

train station

2 Look. Tick or cross. Colour.

1 The aeroplane is flying in the sky. ✔

2 There's a sun on the aeroplane. ☐

3 There are two trains at the train station. ☐

4 There is a sign to the airport. ☐

5 The man at the train station is going sightseeing. ☐

3 Write.

1 I will go swimming on Saturday.
I'll go swimming on Saturday.
2 She will walk to school.
______
3 They will fly to Spain tonight.
______
4 We will meet at the train station tomorrow.
______
5 He will make a sandwich for lunch.
______
6 I will go to the castle this afternoon.
______

4 Write.

1 I 'll buy (buy) you a new phone.
2 My brother ______ (make) you a sandwich.
3 We ______ (go) to the Pyramids in August.
4 Mary and John ______ (build) a new house next year.
5 She ______ (meet) her friend in the town centre.
6 I ______ (clean) my bedroom tomorrow!

5 Write and sing.

airport ~~September~~ September (x3) sightseeing aeroplane journey

We'll see you in September, Mr Smith.
We'll see you in ______, Mrs Jones.
We can't stay. We're on holiday.
So, bye bye! See you later. Off we go!

Let's go to the ______!
Let's fly on the ______!
Let's take a ______ far away!
We'll go ______! We'll take photos!
We'll have lots of fun!
And when we come home,
we'll tell you all we've done.

We'll see you in ______,
Mr Smith.
We'll see you in ______,
Mrs Jones.
We can't stay. We're on
holiday.
So, bye bye! See you later. Off
we go!

Lesson 3

1 Circle.

1
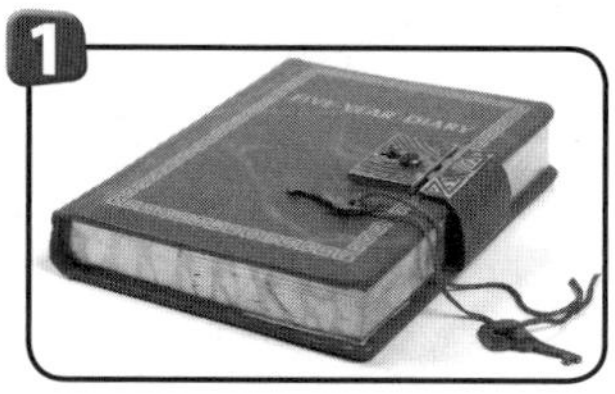
diary / fun

2

stamp / diary

3

stamp / trip

4

postcard / trip

5

fun / postcard

6

present / go shopping

7

present / go shopping

2 Write.

stamp diary postcard ~~go shopping~~ presents fun trip

1 I often go shopping with my mum.
2 I write in my ________ every day.
3 I get lots of ________ on my birthday.
4 This summer we are going to go on a ________ to the beach. It will be ________.
5 I will write a ________ on holiday. I will send it to my friend.
6 I will buy a ________ for my postcard.

3 Write.

1

I'll eat oranges.

I won't eat crisps.

2

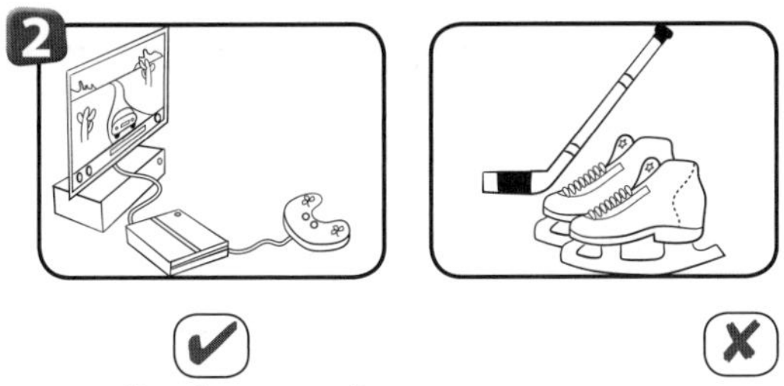

He'll play video games.

He ____________ ice hockey.

3

We'll go hiking.

We ____________ camping.

4

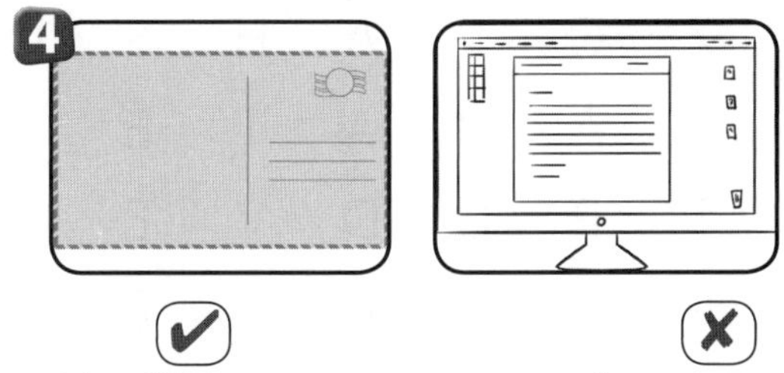

She'll write a postcard.

She ____________ an email.

4 Write.

1 I won't do (do) my homework now.
2 Sally ________________ (go) shopping tomorrow.
3 Mark and Will ________________ (play) football on Sunday.
4 Mum ________________ (cook) at the weekends.
5 My brother ________________ (read) books.
6 Jane ________________ (visit) her grandma this week.

5 Write and say.

Next summer

Go on a trip to Egypt.
Visit my aunt.
See the Pyramids.
Eat Egyptian food.
Swim in the sea.
Buy presents for my friends.

Next summer

She'll go on a trip to Egypt.

____

____

____

____

____

Review 6 Units 11–12

1 Circle and write.

T	E	J	I	E	H	S	A	H
F	O	U	N	T	A	I	N	O
S	T	A	M	P	D	N	T	T
P	O	S	T	C	A	R	D	E
Z	O	L	A	H	S	D	A	L
F	A	N	A	T	E	B	A	H
S	R	O	D	V	E	I	A	H
P	A	V	E	M	E	N	T	E
Z	O	L	E	S	I	G	N	G
A	E	R	O	P	L	A	N	E

1 

bin

2 

____

3 

____

4 

____

5 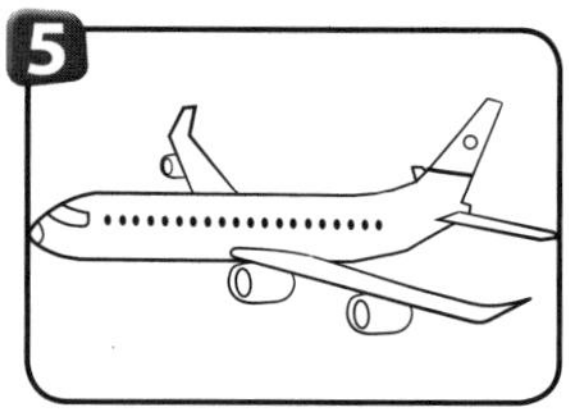

____

6 

____

7 

____

8 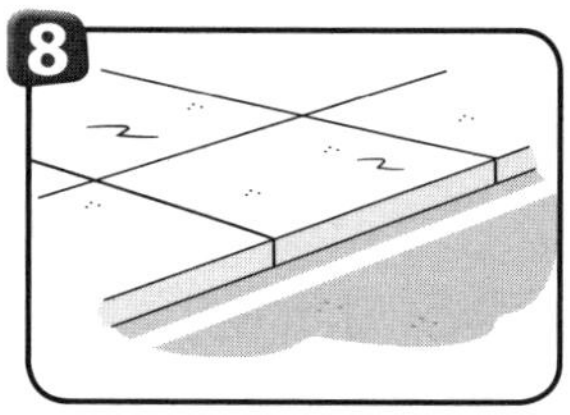

____

2 Order and write.

1 shopping / not / going / to / go / I'm
I'm not going to go shopping.

2 meet/ we / are / ? / to / going / you
____

3 going / she's / to / walk / the / train station / to
____

4 leave / ? / is / going / to / she
____

5 they're / left / to / turn / going / not
____

3 Circle.

He will / **won't** write a postcard.

Pat **will** / **won't** visit his grandma on Saturday.

Harry **will** / **won't** go shopping now.

Mum and Dad **will** / **won't** go sightseeing.

4 Read and write.

~~straight~~	turn (x2)	train	on	aeroplane	cross	castle

How do I get to the train station?
Go straight on, then ________ left at the museum. It's opposite the museum. You can catch a ________ from there.

How do I get to the castle?
Go straight ________, then turn right at the fountain. The ________ is opposite the airport.

How do I get to the airport?
________ the road. Turn right and then ________ left. You can catch an ________ from the airport.

5 Write about you.

____

____

____

____

____

____

____

____

PROJECT 1 On the Farm

1 Count and write.

1 wocs three cows
2 hieknscc ______
3 heesp ______
4 skucd ______
5 aotg ______
6 rotract ______
7 rsohe ______
8 rearfm ______

2 Find a big piece of paper. Draw and colour your dream farm.

Write what you've got in your farm.

3 Bring your drawing to school. Talk to a partner about your farm.

PROJECT 2

Family Time

1 Write an adjective from the box under each picture.

happy sad angry tired hungry ~~thirsty~~

1 

thirsty

3 

5 

2 

4 

6 

2 Make a six-panel booklet. Look for a picture for each adjective in Activity 1.

1 

Take a piece of A4 paper.

2 

Fold it into three equal sections.

3 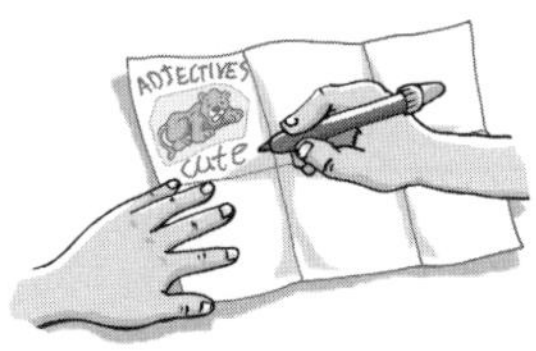

Write ADJECTIVES on the first panel then stick on your picture and write the adjective.

4 

Stick a picture in each panel of your booklet. Then write the adjectives under the pictures.

3 Bring your booklet to school. Talk to a partner about your pictures.

At Home

1 Describe the dining room in the picture to your partner. Use the words in the box. Colour.

door	stairs	table	wall	window
floor	bookshelf	rug	toy box	

2 Look again at the picture. Write answers to these questions.

1 Where is the cat? ______________________________

2 How many windows are there? ______________________

3 Where is the bookshelf? __________________________

3 Find a big piece of paper. Draw and colour your living room, or your dream dining room.

4 Bring your picture to school and show it to your friends.

PROJECT 4

What Do You Eat?

1 Look and answer the questions.

1 How much fruit is on the table? There's a lot of fruit on the table.

2 Are there any oranges on the table? ______

3 Is there any sugar on the table? ______

4 How many sandwiches are on the table? ______

5 Is there any yoghurt on the table? ______

6 Are there any fizzy drinks on the table? ______

2 Draw a picture of a table with lots of different food and drink on it.

3 Work in pairs. Ask and answer questions about your pictures.

PROJECT 5 What's it Like Outside?

1 Write the months in the correct order.

March ~~December~~ June May ~~January~~ August
September July November February October April

1 January
2 ______
3 ______
4 ______
5 ______
6 ______
7 ______
8 ______
9 ______
10 ______
11 ______
12 December

2 Complete these sentences with months.

1 My birthday is in ______.
2 There's snow in ______.
3 It's windy in ______.
4 There are lots of flowers in ______.

3 Make a calendar.

1 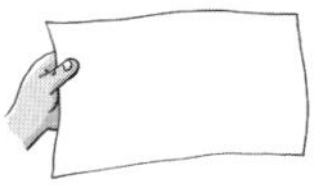

Take a piece of A4 paper.

2 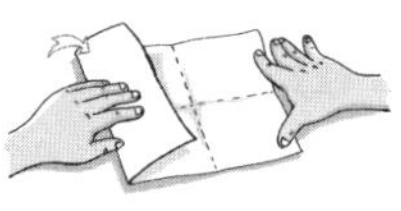

Fold it into three equal sections.

3 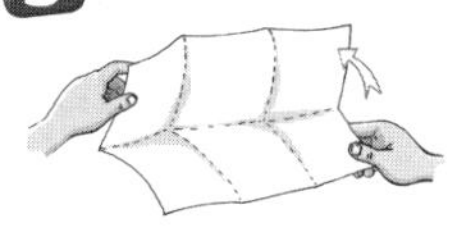

Fold it in half, and then open it so you have six sections on each side.

4 

Write the names of the months at the top of each section.

4 Write some important things that happen in each month.

my birthday, Mum's birthday, summer holiday

5 Bring your calendar to school and show it to your friends.

PROJECT
6 Let's Go!

1 Look and write what they can do.

1 

She can ice-skate.

3 

____

5 

____

2 

____

4 

____

6 

____

2 Write two things that you can do and two things that you can't do.

1 I can ________________

2 ________________

3 I can't ________________

4 ________________

3 Work in pairs. Choose four activities (for example: *dancing, cooking, a sport*) and mime two you can do, and two you can't do. Practise your mimes.

4 Do your mimes for another pair.

Jobs

1 Look and write the jobs.

1
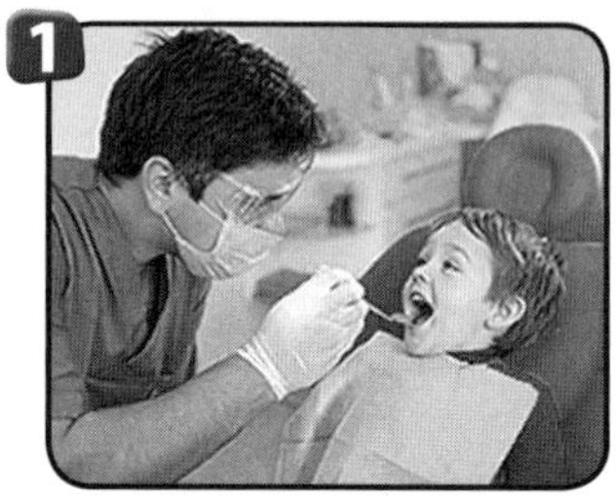

He's a dentist.

3

5
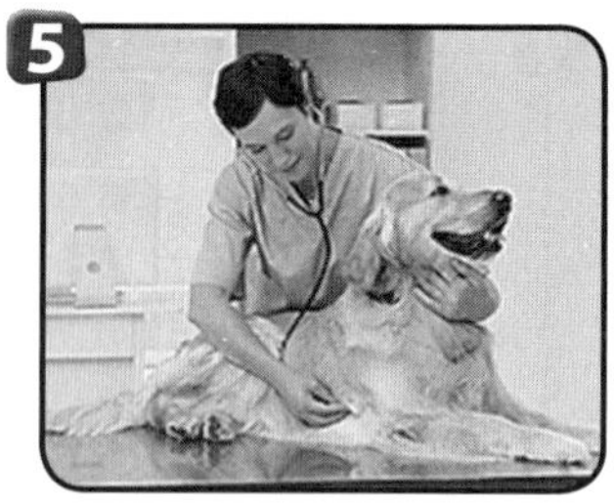

2

4

6

2 Which jobs do you like? Which jobs don't you like?

I like

I dont like

3 What do you want to be when you're older?

I

4 Work in pairs. Decide how to mime six different jobs. Practise your mimes.

Technology

1 Talk about the phones with your partner. Use the words in the box.

new big screen apps old small
quick send emails slow touch

Yes, you can touch Phone 2's screen and it has lots of apps.

Phone 2's screen is bigger than Phone 1's screen.

2 Look again at the phones. Write answers to these questions.

1 Which phone can you share photos on? ______________________

2 Which phone do you need a password for? ___________________

3 Which phone has buttons? ______________________________

3 Draw and colour a picture of a different phone. Think about what it's got and hasn't got.

4 Bring your picture to school. Tell your friends about your phone.

Before Our Time

1 Look and answer the questions.

1

Tyrannosaurus Rex

2

Sauropod

3

Pterodactyl

1 Which dinosaur do you think was a meat-eater?

____

2 Which dinosaur do you think was the biggest?

____

3 Which dinosaur do you think could fly?

____

4 Which dinosaur is your favourite?

____

2 Draw and colour a picture of a different dinosaur. Find out about its food and where it lived (for example: *in the trees, in the water*).

3 Bring your picture to school. Tell your friends about your dinosaur.

PROJECT 10

Cool Places

1 Read the story.

1

Paul got up early yesterday morning.

2

He ate his breakfast and then he went out.

3

Paul wanted to watch birds. First, he went to the forest.

4

He saw a lot of birds in the trees and he took some photos.

5

Next, Paul went to the river. He watched the ducks and some different birds in the water.

6

Then Paul went home for lunch. He was very happy.

2 Draw some pictures and write a story about a happy day.

3 Bring your story to school and let your friends read it. Read their stories.

Keep it Clean

1 Look at the map and answer the questions.

1 How do I get from John's house to the school?

Turn right, cross the road and there it is.

2 How do I get from the train station to the museum?

3 How do I get from the restaurant to the cinema?

4 How do I get from John's house to the train station?

2 Draw a map of some streets in your town. Show where some places are.

3 Bring your map to school. Work in pairs. Ask and answer questions about your maps.

On Holiday

1 Read and write.

Emma's Diary

Next summer, I'll go on a long j o u r n e y. I'll fly to Japan in a big a__________. I won't stay in a h_____, I'll stay with my Japanese friend, Aiko. She'll make me delicious Japanese food. I'll go si___________ and I'll send lots of p_______s. I'll go sh_______ for presents, too. It'll be hot and sunny in Japan and I'll have lots of f_n.

2 Make a diary.

1

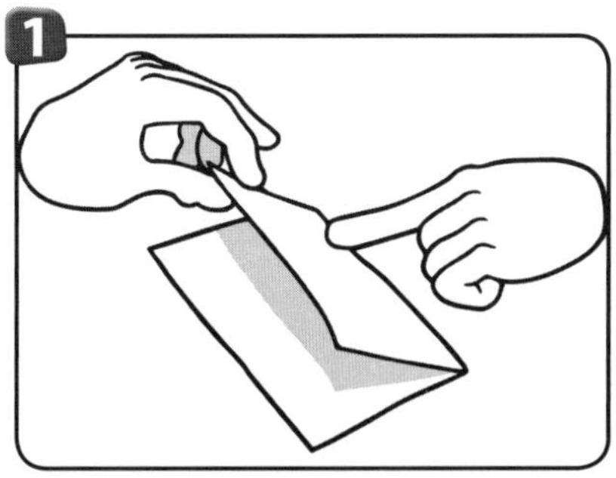

2

3 Write about your dream journey and draw a picture.

4 Bring your diary to school for your friends to read. Read their diaries.

Drawing page

Drawing page

Credits

16(tl) Bold Stock/Unlisted Images; **42(d)** Corbis/Jupiterimages; **86(tm)** Beau Lark/Corbis

© Alamy: 16 Inga Spence; **22(tl)** Blend Images; **37(bl)** Arletta Cwalina; **45** imageBROKER; **56(br)** ZUMA Press Inc; **57(b)** MBI; **74(br)** Editorial; **75(bl)** MBI; **78(bml)** Jan Wlodarczyk; **78(br)** Geogphotos

© Getty Images: 22(tm) Jose Luis Pelaez Inc; **26(f)** James Woodson; **28(e)** ImagesBazaar; **30(tr)** Glow Decor; **30(tm)** Andreas Kuehn; **34(tl)** C Squared Studios; **46(tl)** Neustockimages; **46(ml)** Henrik Sorensen; **46(bl)** Kaisersosa67; **46(mr)** FatCamera; **47(e)** Tetra Images/Brand X Pictures; **51** Hero Images; **53(bl)** Johner Images; **56(bl)** Westend61; **56(tr)** Terry Vine; **57(br)** Daniela Solomon/ Moment; **58(b)** Caiaimage/Chris Ryan; **61(tl)** Image Source; **64(tr)** Rubberball/Mike Kemp; **64(mr)** JGI/Jamie Grill; **64(br)** Rubberball/ Mike Kemp; **66(b)** Sharon Vos-Arnold; **73** Patti McConville/Photographer's Choice; **78(bl)** John and Tina Reid; **86(tr)** Aurelie and Morgan David de Lossy; **86(br)** Ambre Haller; **90(tl)** BraunS; **90(ml)** Jose Luis Pelaez Inc; **94(tmr)** Fuse; **94(bm)** Susie Adams; **104(bl)** Westend61

© iStockphoto: 19 G Lancia; **15(d)** Tirc83; **15(e)** LivingImages; **27** Sonyae; **78(bl)** Wundervisuals

©Robert Harding: 42(g) Christian Kober; **42(k)** Juice Images; **54(e)** Ken Gillham

© Shutterstock: 6 Klara Viskova; **10** Katerina Davidenko; **13** Katerina Davidenko; **14(tl)** Eric Isselee; **14(bl)** Valentina_S; **14(tm)** Mariait; **14(bm)** Eric Isselee; **14(tr)** Eric Isselee; **14(br)** Aksenova Natalya; **15(a)** Muellek Josef; **15(b)** Bronwyn Photo; **15(c)** Cheryl Casey; **15(f)** Zurijeta; **16(tr)** Elenamiv; **16(mr)** Catalin Petolea; **16(br)** PopTika; **16(ml)** Taina Sohlman; **16(bl)** Africa Studio; **18(tr)** SOMMAI; **18(br)** Rodimov; **18(tm)** Lucian Coman; **18(bm)** Niran Phonruang; **18(tl)** 2xSamara.com; **18(bl)** Scott Richardson; **18** Zoom Team; **22(tr)** Eric Isselee; **22(bl)** Jaromir Chalabala; **22(bm)** Eric Isselee; **22(br)** Uber Images; **24(tl)** 3445128471; **24(tm)** Pikul Noorod; **24(tr)** Kuttelvaserova Stuchelova; **24(bl)** Hal_P; **24(bm)** Gosphotodesign; **24(br)** Ladybirdstudio; **25** Ruslan Guzov; **26** Purino; **26(a)** 2xSamara.com; **26(b)** Lucian Coman; **26(c)** Jaromir Chalabala; **26(d)** Niran Phonruang; **26(e)** Eric Isselee; **26(g)** Eric Isselee; **28(a)** Nailia Schwarz; **28(b)** Breadmaker; **28(c)** Villedieu Christophe; **28(d)** Artazum; **28(f)** Who is Danny; **29(tl)** Andreja Donko; **29(ml)** Kati Finell; **29(bl)** Elenamiv; **29(tr)** Nattakit Jeerapatmaitree; **29(mr)** Jenpol Sumatchaya; **29(br)** EcoPrint; **30(tl)** Mikhail Rulkov; **30(bl)** Science Photo; **30(bm)** Gappic; **30(bl)** Hung Chung Chih; **31(a)** Anatoly Tiplyashin; **31(b)** Africa Studio; **31(c)** Kibri_ho; **31(d)** Taina Sohlman; **31(e)** Billion Photos; **31(f)** Jurgita Genyte; **33(tl)** TTphoto; **33(tm)** Smereka; **33(tr)** David Papazian; **33(bl)** Paul Looyen; **33(bm)** Zhannaprokopeva; **33(br)** Petr Jilek; **34(ml)** Drozdowski; **34(bl)** JeniFoto; **34(tr)** Maks Narodenko; **34(mr)** Ilya D. Gridnev; **34(br)** Hurst Photo; **37(tl)** Matt Ragen; **37(mtl)** Mashe; **37(mtr)** Matjaz Preseren; **37(mbl)** Valentina_G; **37(mbr)** Studio 1231; **37(br)** Enrico Jose; **38(a)** Abramova Elena; **38(b)** StudioByTheSea; **38(c)** Stockforlife; **38(d)** Homydesign; **38(e)** Angelo Gilardelli; **39** Nitr; **42(a)** Nuamfolio; **42(b)** LilKar; **42(c)** Zyankarlo; **42(e)** MALOVICHKO OLEKSANDR; **42(f)** Rangizzz; **42(h)** Veronika Galkina; **42(i)** Vibrant Image Studio; **42(j)** Tim S Newman; **42(l)** Allexxandar; **43(tmr)** Chubykin Arkady; **43(tr)** BlueOrange Studio; **43(bl)** SunKids; **43(br)** Inc; **43(tml)** MANDY GODBEHEAR; **43(tl)** Jacek Chabraszewski; **46(tr)** Karramba Production; **47(a)** Zurijeta; **47(b)** Archana Bhartia; **47(c)** Nejron Photo; **47(d)** Pirita; **48(tl)** TravnikovStudio; **48(ml)** Creative Travel Projects; **48(bl)** Shooter Bob Square Lenses; **48(tr)** Gorillaimages; **48(br)** Iofoto; **52(tl)** Iofoto; **52(tm)** OHishiapply; **52(tr)** Galyna Andrushko; **52(bl)** Greenland; **52(bm)** Olga Danylenko; **53(tl)** Gladskikh Tatiana; **53(tm)** Alex Egorov; **53(bm)** lightwavemedia; **53(tr)** Monkey Business Images; **53(br)** Ruslana Iurchenko; **54(a)** Simoly; **54(b)** Petr Malyshev; **54(c)** Nikitabuida; **54(d)** Helga Chirk; **54(f)** Greenland; **54(g)** Monkey Business Images; **54(h)** Monkey Business Images; **56(tl)** ESB Professional; **56(ml)** Olesia Bilkei; **57(a)** Kristian Sekulic; **57(c)** Stefan Petru Andronache; **57(d)** ArrowStudio; **57(e)** Dave Gordon; **57(f)** Maksim Shmeljov; **58(a)** Wavebreakmedia; **58(c)** Mkos83; **58(d)** Spass; **58(e)** DeymosHR; **59** Nicholas Piccillo; **60(tl)** Michaeljung; **60(tm)** Andrew Doran; **60(tr)** EML; **60(bl)** Haider Y. Abdulla; **60(bm)** StockLite; **60(br)** Orange Line Media; **61(bl)** Monkey Business Images; **62(a)** Andy Dean Photography; **62(b)** Sergey Peterman; **62(c)** Julia Nikitina; **62(d)** KavardakovA; **62(e)** Roman Samokhin; **62(f)** Julia Nikitina; **63** Blend Images; **64(tl)** Bloomicon; **64(ml)** Yienkeat; **64(bl)** Romvo; **65** Pincasso; **66(t)** Rawpixel.com; **66(mt)** Westend61 Premium; **66(m)** Rebius; **66(mb)** Rzoze19; **67(tl)** Umberto Shtanzman; **67(tm)** Maya Kruchankova; **67(tr)** Adisa; **67(bl)** Oleg Krugliak; **67(bm)** Bfk; **70(tl)** Ozja; **70(tml)** Fototaler; **70(tm)** HomeStudio; **70(tmr)** MriMan; **70(tr)** Avatar_023; **72(tl)** Ajlatan; **72(tm)** Heromen30; **72(tr)** Irencik; **72(bl)** JDCarballo; **72(bm)** Kirillov Alexey; **72(br)** Evgeny Karandaev; **74(tl)** JDCarballo; **74(tr)** Dmitry Naumov; **74(bl)** AlohaHawaii; **75(mbl)** Melanie DeFazio; **75(br)** wavebreakmedia; **75(mbr)** Aleks k; **76(tl)** BCFC; **76(bl)** Agean; **76(tm)** Boris Stroujko; **76(bm)** Dibrova; **76(r)** Vir Ivlev; **78(tl)** Orange Line Media; **78(tm)** Pius Lee; **78(tr)** Ev Thomas; **78(bm)** Chuyuss; **78(br)** Eric Isselee; **78(btr)** Philip Lange; **78(btr)** Luciano Mortula - LGM; **78(bmr)** Seleznev Oleg; **80(a)** Rocharibeiro; **80(b)** Tanasan Sungkaew; **80(c)** Goodluz; **80(d)** MATULEE; **80(e)** Maximumvector; **80(f)** Eva Gattuso; **80(g)** Petch One; **80(h)** Gil C; **80(i)** Julinzy; **84(tl)** VVO; **84(tml)** Tatyana Vyc; **84(tmr)** Val Lawless; **84(tr)** Jorge Salcedo; **84(bl)** Fstockfoto; **84(bm)** Nick Starichenko; **84(br)** Nadiia Gerbish; **86(tl)** Wavebreakmedia; **86(bl)** Colors; **90(bl)** Vadim Georgiev; **90(tr)** Brian A Jackson; **90(mr)** Stock-Asso; **90(br)** Monkey Business Images; **92(tr)** Vaalaa; **92(mr)** Victor Tyakht; **92(tl)** Vibrant Image Studio; **92(ml)** Jointstar; **92(b)** Michaelpuche; **93** Guillermo77; **94(tl)** Ikphotographers; **94(tml)** Ronnachai Palas; **94(tr)** Kamil Macniak; **94(bl)** EtiAmmos; **94(br)** Timothy Hodgkinson; **99(tl)** Gosphotodesign; **99(tm)** 3445128471; **99(tr)** Pikul Noorod; **99(bl)** Kuttelvaserova Stuchelova; **99(bm)** Hal_P; **99(br)** Ladybirdstudio; **103(tl)** TravnikovStudio; **103(bl)** Galyna Andrushko; **103(tm)** Shooter Bob Square Lenses; **103(bm)** Gorillaimages; **103(tr)** Iofoto; **103(br)** Greenland; **104(tl)** Olesia Bilkei; **104(tm)** ESB Professional; **104(bm)** Eddtoro; **104(tr)** Wavebreakmedia; **104(br)** Mazan Xeniya